COMMON CORE CLINICS

Grade 6

English Language Arts

Reading Literature

Common Core Clinics, English Language Arts, Reading Literature, Grade 6
OT250 / 362NA

ISBN-13: 978-0-7836-8481-9

Cover Image: © HuntStock/Photolibrary

Triumph Learning® 136 Madison Avenue, 7th Floor, New York, NY 10016

Printed in the United States of America.

10 9 8 7 6 5 4 3 2 1

ALL ABOUT YOUR BOOK

COMMON CORE CLINICS will help you master important reading skills.

Each lesson has a **Learn About It** box that teaches the idea. A sample passage focuses on the skill. A **graphic organizer** shows you a reading strategy.

Each lesson has a **Try It** passage with **guided reading**.

Higher-Order Thinking Skills

Questions that make you think further about what you read.

Apply It provides **independent practice** for reading passages, answering short-answer questions, and responding to writing prompts.

Table of Contents

Character and Plot

Learn About It

Characters are the people, animals, or other creatures in a story or drama. A **plot** is the sequence of events that tells a story from beginning to end. The **conflict** is the problem that a character must resolve. The **rising action** is the time during which the character works to resolve the problem. The **climax** is the turning point in the story, and it is usually the most exciting part. The **resolution** is the time when the conflict is resolved, which is at the end of the story. As the plot unfolds, the characters respond and change before the conflict is resolved. For example, a timid character may change to act heroically in the story.

Read the passage. As you read, think about how the characters make the plot move forward.

Sly was the most ruthless snake in the forest. The chipmunk family had always lived in fear of him.

But George was tired of living in fear. He tiptoed up behind Sly, and then broke into a run. He leaped over Sly and scurried up a nearby tree. He was safe before Sly had even noticed him.

"Take that, Sly!" said George. "You do not rule this forest!"

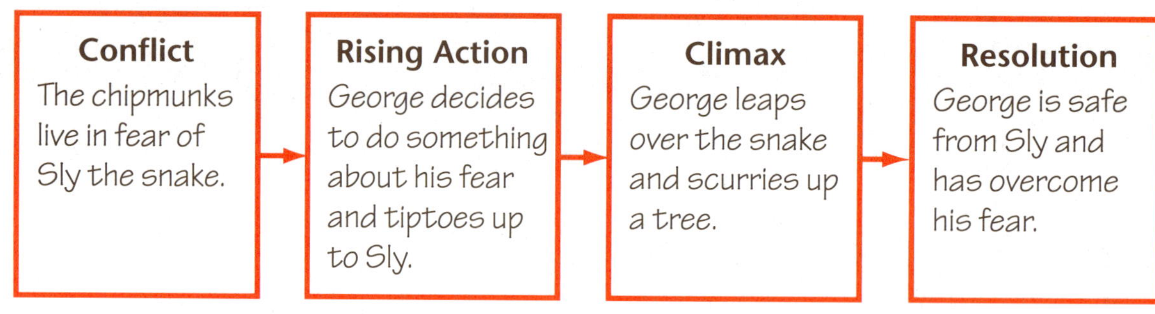

Try It

Read the passage. Underline the character names and words that help you identify elements of plot, such as conflict, rising action, climax, and resolution. Use the questions to help you.

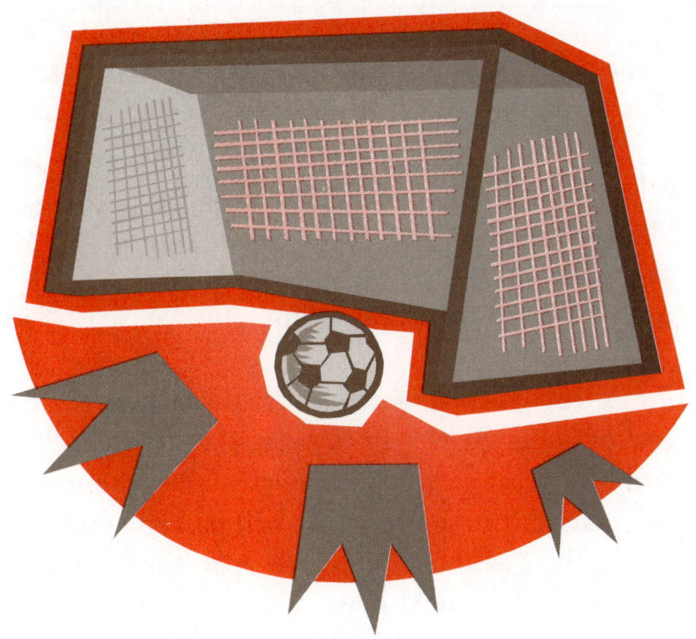

A Tired Soccer Star

When Lori put on her cleats that morning, she was exhausted. She had been up half the night with her crying baby brother. Her parents kept telling Lori to go back to bed, but that was much easier said than done. She had always been a light sleeper, and a screaming baby was definitely not what she needed the night before her big soccer game. She finally just joined her parents in Aaron's bedroom and helped to sing him back to bed.

Now she was paying for it on the soccer field. Her coach called her name and she barely heard it because she was in such a daze. After another call, she finally heard it. They were all calling her name! Lori looked up and saw the ball flying toward her. She sprang into action and thought as quickly as she could. She pulled her knee up to hit the ball and to keep it from passing her on the way to the goal. But her efforts weren't enough. She missed the ball, and it bounced past her. She could hear groans and shrieks from the audience. She looked down in embarrassment. She knew that nobody in the stands would care that she was tired and was up late last night. The players around her rushed for control of the ball.

Which character in the story does Lori blame for being tired during her soccer game?

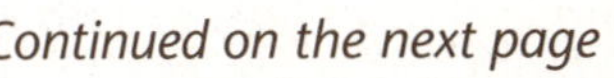
Continued on the next page

Continued from the previous page

She looked around to see people's disapproving looks. But then she noticed her parents and baby brother in the stands. They were here to see her work hard, not to sulk. They were just as tired as she was, she thought to herself. She took another quick peek at them and saw her mother's friendly wave. It was as if she were trying to signal to her that things were not that bad. Lori looked around the field and decided to get her head back into the game. No use letting a little tiredness and a silly mistake get her down.

Lori ran toward the ball and jumped into the game. Her mind sprang back to life and she no longer felt tired. Two of her teammates cheered her name and clapped for her. They knew she was back in the game. "Over here!" she yelled to her friend Mackenzie. "I'm open!" Just then, Mackenzie passed her the ball and Lori kept control of the ball until she nearly reached the opposing team's goal. She heard the stands erupt with cheers.

What is the rising action of the story?

For a split second, she wondered whether she should pass the ball to Mackenzie to take a shot at the goal or if she should try to make the shot herself.

"Do it!" she heard Mackenzie yell next to her. "Take the shot!" Lori took all the strength she had and focused it on getting that ball past the goalie. She shut her eyes as she made the final kick. She was almost afraid to open them again, but she knew she had made it when she heard the crowd roar.

On the way home from the game, Lori fell asleep in the car next to her baby brother. They had both made the most of the day, and now it was time for a nap.

Why does Lori decide to work hard and "get her head back into the game"?

Apply It

Read the drama. Ask yourself questions about the characters and how they change as the plot moves toward a resolution. Answer the questions that follow.

Friend or Foe?

Act I Scene 1

Setting: Curtain rises, showing two friends doing their homework together. Jason and Nick are both boys about 12 years old.

JASON: (*frustrated*) I just don't understand this homework, Nick. There are too many fractions, and they make my head spin.

NICK: (*encouraging*) Don't worry, Jason. Just take each step one at a time, as if it's the only problem you are looking at. Then, do the next step when you're ready.

JASON: Well, that sounds easy, but this is really hard stuff. Can't I look at your paper and see how you did it?

NICK: I can help you, but you can't look at my paper. That would be cheating.

JASON: Why would that be cheating? We're not taking a test. This is our homework. We're supposed to learn the right way to do things. You're a really good math student, so you should let me look at your paper.

NICK: Sorry, dude. I can't let you copy my paper. I am going to help you, step by step. You'll get the same answers if you do it right, and you'll learn at the same time.

JASON: (*angry*) You think I'm just trying to copy you? I can't believe you. I don't even want your help anymore. (*stands up*)

NICK: (*surprised*) Hold on there, buddy! What's going on? I am trying to help you. You told me the work was hard, and I offered to help you. But now you're angry at me for not just giving you my paper? Am I supposed to just give you my homework because you're my friend?

JASON: Well I thought I was your friend. But a friend of mine would let me look at his homework.

NICK: (*angry*) Well, a friend of mine would not demand that I give him my homework answers!

JASON: Well, then I guess we are not friends! (*storms out*)

Continued on the next page 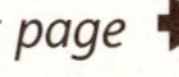

Continued from the previous page

Act I Scene 2

Setting: Nick and Jason are in their own homes, talking on the phone to each other, a stage curtain hangs between them to divide the set.

NICK: Jason, I hope we can be friends. This math thing is really not a good thing for us to argue over. It's not worth it, you know? I think that if you want to look at my paper, I can help you to understand the answers.

JASON: I know you didn't mean to be mean or anything. I guess it's a good idea if you just help to explain the homework to me. I think I was just feeling upset about not understanding it.

NICK: Don't worry. It really took me a while to understand fractions also. But when you practice, it really gets easy. You'll feel good about it pretty soon.

JASON: Well, we'll see about that. Do you want to come over after dinner and help me? My mom said that you can if I finish all my other homework before you come over.

NICK: Sounds like a plan, man. I'm already finished with my homework, so I will be happy to help.

JASON: Thanks. You really are a friend.

Answer these questions about "Friend or Foe?" Write your answers in complete sentences.

1. What is the main conflict in the drama?

___

___

2. How can you describe the relationship between the characters?

___

___

3. What is the rising action in the drama?

___

___

4. How are the characters involved in the plot's climax?

___

___

5. What is the resolution of the drama?

___

___

Supporting an Analysis of Text

Learn About It

When you **analyze** text, you think about it to help you to understand it better. As you think about what you have read, look for information in the story. Look at word choice, character development, and plot. Text that comes right from the story is called **evidence**. Use evidence to help you support your analysis.

Read the passage. As you read, think about text that can help you analyze and understand what the author is saying.

Mom knew that we couldn't have a puppy unless everyone was ready to do his or her share to take care of it. She made a list of duties that needed to be done. She listed feeding, walking, bathing, and playing as important jobs. She knew we all had to take turns to make sure that all of the jobs were fair.

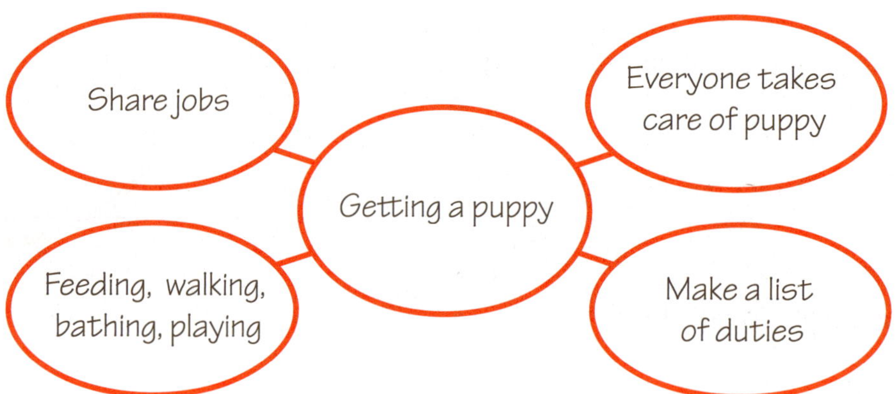

Analysis: It takes a lot of hard work and cooperation to take care of a puppy.

Try It

Read the passage. Underline evidence from the text that helps you understand what you are reading. This will help you to analyze what you read. Use the questions to help you.

Jake's Dream

Jake had a dream that he climbed Mt. Everest—again. He loved this dream. He had a backpack full of food and water and was ready to climb to the top of the world's tallest mountain. Because this was a dream, Jake never had to worry about the fact that this would actually be a very, very difficult journey. In reality, he would need to be an extremely skilled hiker and mountain climber. He would have to know how to scale dangerous cliffs covered in ice. He would have to endure threatening temperatures that could chill him to the bone. But the dream did not require any of those preparations. Jake was just a man on an adventure. In fact, in these dreams, his little dog, Bucky, always followed three steps behind him, wagging his tail.

Today's dream was just a little bit different from the others that Jake has had. Today, Jake took off from the base of the mountain and flew up to the top. He soared, Bucky in his arms, up and above the clouds. He gazed at mountains next to him and horizons that seemed a lifetime away. When he reached the tip of the mountaintop, he fluttered like a hummingbird and gently landed in the snow. This was the best dream yet, he thought to himself. He let Bucky down on the ground and Bucky immediately dug a hole in the snow to make a fort for the two of them. They stayed in the fort for several days as a storm passed overhead. Instead of being exposed to the elements, they were safe and warm in the snow fort.

Why is this dream about Mt. Everest different from Jake's other dreams about Mt. Everest?

Soon after the storm passed, Jake and Bucky came out of their snow fort and looked at the scenery. It was wonderful to be at the highest point on Earth, looking out to the top of other snow-covered mountaintops. Bucky wagged his tail and Jake took out a doggie snack for him. Then, he unwrapped a sandwich for himself.

They weren't mountain gazing for more than five minutes when they had company at the summit. This had also never happened in Jake's dreams of Mt. Everest. They suddenly found themselves sharing the summit of the mountain with his sister.

"What are you doing up here?" she asked. "You know you are not supposed to walk Bucky outside of the neighborhood," she whined. Jake could not help but wonder how she got up to the top of the mountain just to scold him. He looked at her oddly.

"Why are you here?" he asked.

"I just decided to go out for a walk, and here I am," she replied.

What does Jake's sister do in his dream?

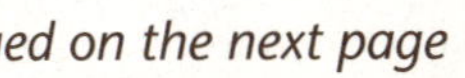
Continued on the next page ➔

Continued from the previous page

"But we are on top of the highest mountain in the world," Jake said. "You can't just take a stroll up here."

"You can if this is a dream," she said. "Now get up and take the dog for a walk. Take him for a walk!" She started to shake on his arm as he sat there at the top of the mountain.

Just then, Jake awoke in his bed at home, with his sister shaking his arm. "Get up," she said. "It's your turn to take the dog for a walk before school!"

What does the dialogue tell you about the characters?

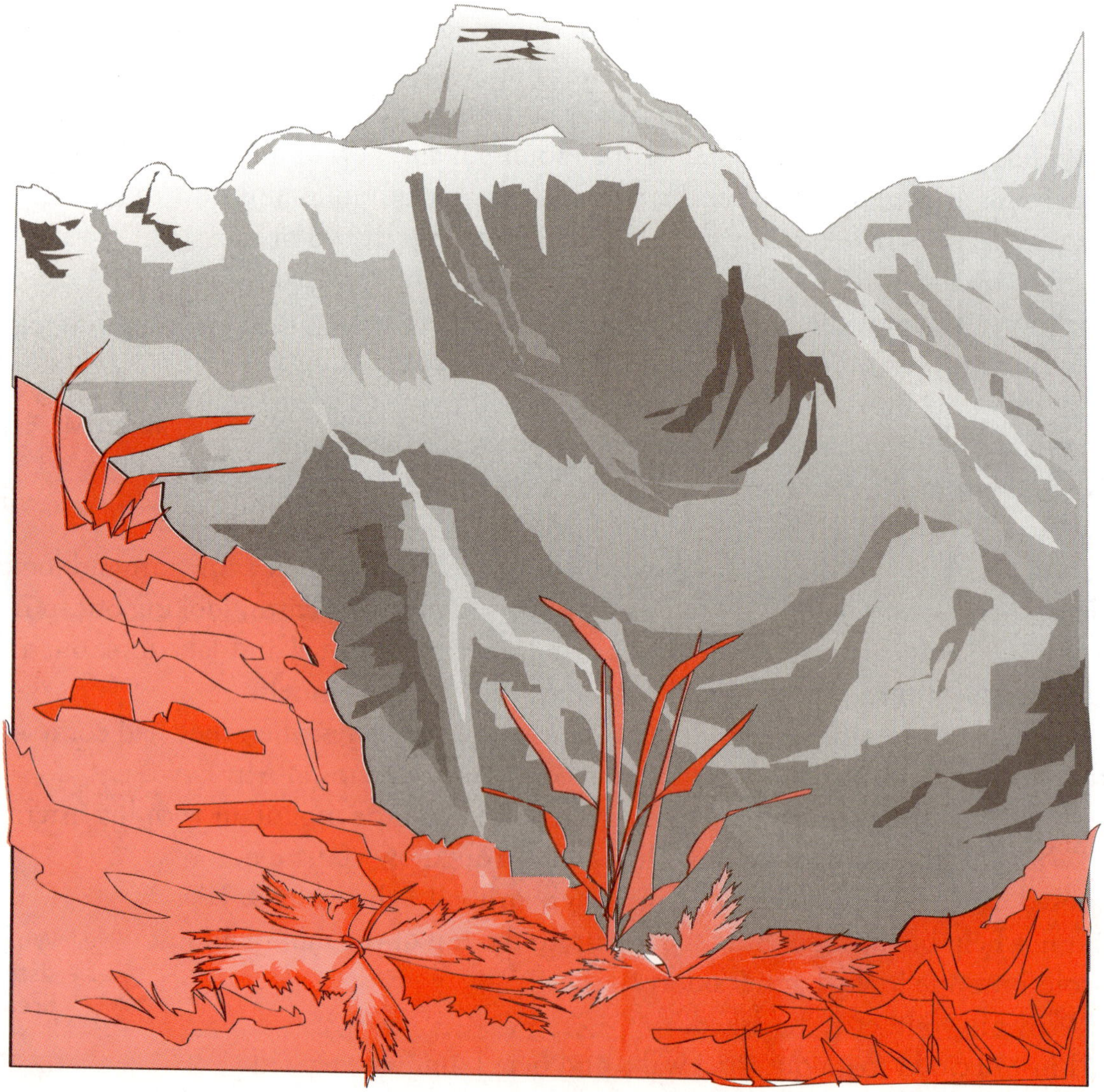

Apply It

Read the passage. Ask yourself questions that will help you to analyze the text. Look for evidence that will help you answer those questions. Answer the questions that follow.

The Baker Sisters

Becky and her sister always had big plans. Their latest idea was to become bakers and open their own bakery. They knew it would be about fifteen years before they could do it for real, but they loved to plan ahead. They made a master list of all of the things they would need for their business. They listed the types of cookies, pies, breads, and cakes that they would like to make for their business. Then they predicted how much they would need in ingredients to bake each item. They decided that they would need 10 tons of flour, 13 tons of sugar, and 15 tons of butter for their bakery. That's not to mention the tons of eggs, oil, nuts, and chocolate they would be using every day. Their eyes sparkled with excitement as they looked at their list. They hoped that this plan would work out. They both loved baking, and a bakery would be so much fun, they thought.

"It would be best if we started our plan right away," said Becky.

"You are right," replied her sister Sarah. "Let's ask Mom and Dad if they will let us buy a ton of flour this year, and then we can buy a ton of sugar next year. Each year we can buy one ton of ingredients and keep it in the garage until we open the bakery," she said excitedly.

"I think even at that rate we won't finish in time," said Becky. "Let's double it and see what they say."

"OK, we'd better get started," said Sarah, rubbing her hands together with excitement.

The girls made a list for their parents to show the tons of ingredients they wanted to buy each year for the next fifteen years, but they were met with laughter instead of excitement. Their parents were not willing to buy any of the ingredients now. They thought the girls should wait until they got much older to start planning in such detail. Their dad said there was a lot to learn in school that could change their plans. They might learn better ways to run a business. They might learn new ways to buy ingredients that would be better than buying tons at a time. They also thought it was important to have a bakery to store their ingredients in a rather than to keep it in the garage for so long.

Continued on the next page ➔

Continued from the previous page

"I guess he is right," said Becky with a sigh. "But wouldn't you just love to start planning for the business now?"

"Oh, I sure would," said Sarah. "Hey, maybe we can start a tiny business right now without having a bakery. Maybe Mom and Dad would let us bake some cookies in our own kitchen and sell them to people we know. It would be so much fun," she said with her usual excitement. "Do you want to start with chocolate chip cookies? I can get some ingredients right from the cabinet right now!"

"Great idea," replied Becky.

Answer these questions about "The Baker Sisters." Write your answers in complete sentences.

1. What is Becky and Sarah's dream?

2. What do the girls plan to do to prepare for their business now?

3. Why do they decide to change their plan?

4. What do the girls decide to do instead?

5. Are Becky and Sarah reasonable characters?

Learn About It

A **theme** is the main idea, moral, or message in a piece of writing. The reader must **analyze** the story in order to decide what the theme is. Thinking about the character's actions and the plot help the reader to decide about theme. The reader can also look for repeating ideas in a story.

Read the passage. As you read, try to decide what the theme of the story is.

The ants worked hard all summer collecting food for winter. They liked to be prepared and comfortable during the long hard winter. The grasshoppers played all summer and did not think about saving food for harder times.

When winter came, the ants stayed warm in their underground homes and had enough food for everyone. The grasshoppers came calling, hungry and tired. Their poor planning had cost them dearly.

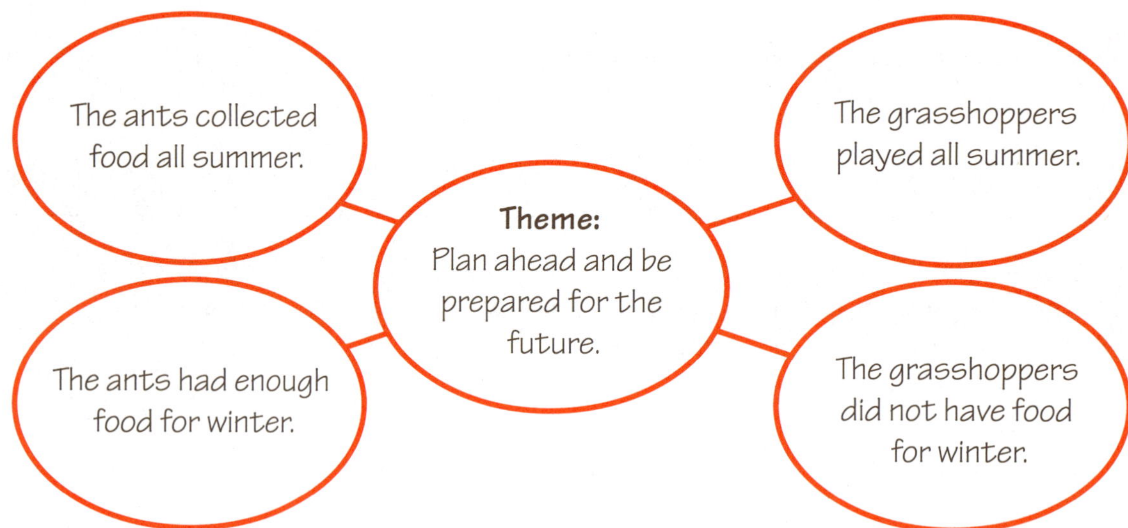

Try It

Read the passage. Underline phrases that help you determine the theme of the passage. Use the questions to help you.

Marcus Cooks

No one in the Diaz family could cook quite like Marcus. When his brothers and sisters would open the cabinet for a snack, Marcus would instead want to chop some vegetables, grate some cheese, and work with Nona to cook up a family meal and get the kitchen smelling like a Mexican restaurant.

Nona knew that Marcus had a special talent for cooking early in life. The most important clue was that Marcus was interested in cooking in the kitchen. When the other children were out playing in the yard, Nona stood at the counter with her little grandson by her side, breaking green beans in half and throwing them into a big bowl of water to rinse for the night's dinner. The other children teased Marcus and told him that he should be playing sports like a boy instead of cooking like a girl. But Marcus didn't listen at all to what the other children said.

Instead, he laid out a family feast for his brothers and sisters. They ate the food without thinking twice about what Marcus did to make it. Then one day, Marcus and Nona decided to go to a cooking exhibit in the big city. They took the train together and chatted about what they might see and learn about the exhibit. They stayed in a fancy hotel in the city and ate at a wonderful restaurant in the hotel. Marcus could not be happier to spend the weekend with his grandmother and to learn a few new things about cooking at the same time.

But the children at home were far from happy. There was no one to cook their meals that weekend! Their parents were busy with cleaning the house as they usually did during the weekend, and they ordered some take-out food for the children. As soon as they started eating the food, they missed Marcus and Nona terribly. The food was heavy, unseasoned, and nothing like the delicious food that Marcus would prepare for them.

Even their parents noticed the difference in flavor. They tried a different restaurant the next night in hopes that the food would be tastier. The family sat around the table with pouts on their faces.

How do Marcus's brothers and sisters feel about his cooking at the beginning of the story?

Continued on the next page ➔

Continued from the previous page

"When are Marcus and Nona coming home?" asked the littlest child, Annabelle.

"They'll be back at the end of the weekend," assured their mother. "I'll bet you are all missing their delicious cooking right about now. They do a great thing for this family, don't they?" she asked. The children all sat in silence, staring at their plates.

What happens in the plot that makes Marcus's brothers and sisters change their minds about Marcus?

After dinner, the older children talked outside at the swing sets. "What if we asked Nona to teach us how to cook?" Sonya wondered. "Do you think we could learn as much as Marcus did?"

"I'm not sure," replied Jorge. "I wonder how long it took Marcus to learn all that. He's been cooking since he was a little kid," he said.

When Marcus returned from the exhibit in the big city, he felt happy and relieved. "I don't care what you guys say about cooking," he said, as he entered the house. "It's a great thing that everyone should learn!" And with that, his brothers and sisters wholeheartedly agreed.

What is the theme of the passage?

Apply It

Read the passage. Think about how the author's words help you to understand the story's theme. Answer the questions that follow.

adapted from

The Olive Tree and the Fig Tree

by Aesop

For many years, an olive tree and a fig tree stood side by side in a field. The olive tree had always made fun of the fig tree and ridiculed it during their long days standing side by side. The olive tree bragged about staying green with bushy leaves all year long, while the fig tree changed with the season. The fig tree was green in summer, and then its leaves changed color in the fall. The leaves finally fell to the ground, leaving the fig tree bare and exposed to the cold weather. The olive tree laughed at the fig tree's winter appearance and mocked it for becoming ugly and bare.

"I can keep warm during the winter with my blanket of leaves," said the olive tree. "You, on the other hand, are bare and exposed to winter's terrible blows. The wind and snow fall directly on you. How can you bear such difficult treatment by the seasons? Just when you need them most for protection, your leaves fall to the ground to blanket the grass. You are left with nothing, cold and barren in the field."

"This has always been the way that fig trees live," replied the fig tree, in defense of itself. "I am used to the cold winters, and it makes springtime and new growth that much more beautiful. I enjoy the seasons here in this field."

Winter's cold temperatures and windy weather came to see the trees in the field. Then, a rare event happened in the field, even for the winter season. A large snowstorm brought several feet of snow to the land. At first, the olive tree was cozy and warm under the blanket of snow and leaves. Then another storm came and added more snow upon the trees and the field. Soon the olive tree was straining under the weight of the snow on top of its leaves. The branches of the tree sank lower and lower. Large branches soon broke under the weight of the snow. The olive tree wished for relief. It suddenly understood how the fig tree could make it through the long winter unharmed.

Continued on the next page ➜

Continued from the previous page

The fig tree, bare and exposed, was certainly cold during the storms. But its bare branches caused the snow to fall right through to the ground. Its branches were safe, and it stood as tall and proud as it had on any summer day. The fig tree looked at the olive tree with sadness. "I wish I could help you," it said to the olive tree. "You look like you are suffering. Your branches may all be gone soon."

"Your bare branches help with something," said the olive tree. "I am sorry I mocked you. What I would give now for some bare branches to keep this snow from collecting on me."

Answer these questions about "The Olive Tree and the Fig Tree." Write your answers in complete sentences.

1. What is the theme of the story?

2. How do the olive tree's actions help you to figure out the theme?

3. How do the fig tree's actions help you to figure out the theme?

4. What happens in the plot that changes the direction of the story?

5. What lesson did the characters learn in the story? Use examples from the text to explain your answer.

Summarize Text

Learn About It

When you **summarize** a passage or text, you tell in your own words what the story was mainly about. You include the most important information about plot, characters, setting, and theme. When giving a summary, do not include your personal opinions about the story. A summary should not include judgments about the story.

Read the passage. As you read, think about how you can summarize the passage in your own words.

When the spaceship took off over the playing field, Maggie and Cleo waved goodbye. They enjoyed their visit with Marlin the Martian. He often visited Earth and brought the kids Martian cookies and cakes. In return, the girls offered him odd Earth foods, such as popcorn and tofu. Then, Marlin grabbed some rocks and tree bark and took off in his ship.

Detail	Detail	Detail
Marlin takes off in his spaceship.	Marlin brings space foods.	Maggie and Cleo give Marlin Earth foods.

Summary
Marlin the Martian is friends with Maggie and Cleo.

Try It

Read the passage. Underline phrases that help you summarize the passage. Use the questions to help you.

Cleaning with Meaning

Javier had been asked to clean his room so many times that it made his head spin. The truth was that he did not know what to do with all of the junk that cluttered his room. His mother would send him to his room to clean, and he would end up pushing things under his bed, and stuffing his drawers and closets with the objects he was meant to be tidying up.

Which ideas are most important to the story?

Sure, he knew where to put his clean laundry and dirty laundry, and he knew where to put his homework and schoolbooks. But beyond that, he wasn't sure where to put anything. His grandfather always gave him newspaper cutouts from comics, and articles he thought Javier would like to read. Where would something like that go? He also got new toys from birthday party goody bags. Where would he put the little pencils, erasers, toy cars, and playing cards that were always coming into the house? He also didn't know what to do with models he had built with his dad. Airplanes, ships, and trains sat all along the shelves and dressers. That made it impossible to put a new book or notebook down when he entered the room.

Finally, he sought out some help from his mother. "If you can help me to make a place for all of my new things, I promise I will remember in the future where to put stuff. I just don't have room for all the stuff I have. My room will never get clean."

Surprisingly, his mother was happy to help. Javier imagined that she would be angry at him and make him do the chore all by himself. Instead, they spent hours going through each item in his room. First, they made a pile of things that should be kept and things that should be thrown out. Then, they organized the pile of items that he wanted to keep. That night, Javier's dad put three new shelves up on his walls and there was suddenly room for almost everything. Models, books, new toys, old toys, music, and games all had a proper place for the first time. There seemed to be a place for everything. Javier was so happy about how the room looked that he hugged his parents and thanked them for their help.

Continued on the next page ➔

Continued from the previous page

With his room the way he finally wanted it, he was careful to keep it clean every day and make sure all new items had a place to go before they entered the room.

Just as he was about to relax on his bed with a book, Javier's little sister Amelia entered the room. "Can I do my puzzle in here on your floor? It's so clean in here. There's no space in my room to do it."

"No way," warned Javier. "There's no place for that kind of thing in here. Go clean your own room. Let me know if you want some help," he added. "I know some good tricks to finding room for stuff."

Which ideas are least important and not to be included in a summary?

HOTS Analyze

Why do you think Javier is or is not likely to keep his room clean?

Apply It

Read the passage. Think about how you can summarize what you read. Answer the questions that follow.

Stand Tall, Try Not to Fall

Craig had watched his brother ride a skateboard for years. He liked to see the pops and turns he did out on the back patio for practice. He loved the sound of the wheels and deck hitting the pavement in a rhythm: pop, crash, pop, crash, over and over again.

Craig knew it would soon be his turn to take Doug's old skateboard and try it out for himself. The day finally came, and Doug talked patiently with his brother on the back deck. He taught him the terms that were used to refer to each trick, and how to move his feet on the deck to do each trick.

"First, you should just try to stand on the thing without falling off. Stand tall, and try not to fall. If that works, we can take it from there," Doug explained to his brother.

"Sure," said Craig excitedly. But, just as soon as he placed one foot on the skateboard, the wheels took off at high speed and the deck flew out from under him. Craig was down on the ground and scarcely knew what hit him. He had not expected such a problem the first time he stepped foot on the board.

He quickly looked up to see the expression on his brother's face. What surprised him even more than his fall was the fact that his brother was not laughing at him. Instead, he looked concerned.

"Don't worry, it happens," said Doug. "People don't realize that this is a tricky sport. It looks like fun, but it is a lot of work, too." He extended his hand to help his brother off the ground. "Let's try again."

Continued on the next page ➔

Continued from the previous page

That's just what they did. The boys spent most of the afternoon simply getting Craig to balance on the board and make it move by pushing off the ground with one foot. Craig concentrated on every word of advice his brother gave him. When he fell, he got right back up and got back to work.

By the end of the day, Craig was able to skate from one end of the patio to the other without falling. He was proud of his work and knew that if he continued to practice this hard, he would someday be as good as his brother.

After a few hours, Doug went into the house for dinner as the sun began to set over the patio. Craig kept skating and skating, slowly gaining confidence with every trip across the pavement. Yes, he thought to himself, this will take some time, but it will be worth the effort.

Answer these questions about "Stand Tall, Try Not to Fall." Write your answers in complete sentences.

1. Write a summary of the first paragraph of the passage.

2. What are three details that are not important enough to be included in a summary of the passage?

3. When writing a summary, why is it important not to give your opinion about Craig or his brother?

4. Write a summary of the passage.

LESSON 5

Drawing and Supporting Inferences

Learn About It

Sometimes the author explains things clearly for the reader. Other times the reader must draw an **inference** about what is being read. To make an inference, you must think about what you already know and what the author tells you. These ideas together help a reader to make inferences and analyze a text.

Read the passage. As you read, think how you can draw an inference about the text.

George sat on the living room couch and put his foot up on a cushion. He leaned back and sank into the couch with relief.

"Here's some ice to put on that ankle," said his mother as she walked into the room.

"Thanks," said George.

"It was a good game, but you have to be more careful," she said.

What I Read		What I Know		My Inference
George is relaxing on the couch with his foot up. His mother gives him ice for his ankle. George was in a game.	→	Playing sports means having to be careful so you do not get hurt.	→	George probably hurt his ankle playing sports.

Try It

Read the passage. Underline phrases that help you to draw inferences about what you read and to support your inferences. Use the questions to help you.

Jessica's Decision

Jessica stood at the door of the candy shop and gazed inside. She saw her mother smiling as always, waiting on customers. She knew her mother would not get out of work for another hour. How could she wait that long to tell her? She turned back to look at her dad sitting in the car. He was impatiently waiting for her to get in so they could pick up some last-minute groceries before dinner.

"I'm coming," she said to her dad, after he beeped the car horn for the third time. Should she tell him about her test score? If she did, he was bound to get angry, and she would still have to repeat the whole story again when her mother got home.

What does Jessica feel nervous about telling her parents?

She got into the car and slammed the door shut behind her. "Sorry, Dad," she said. "I guess I was daydreaming again. Let's go shopping for dinner. I think we just need some peppers and onions to make the chili."

"I don't know what is going on with you, Jessica. You looked like you were in a daze over there. I honked the horn twice, and you never even heard me. There must be something weighing on your mind."

"Yeah, maybe you are right," Jessica answered. "I have to think about what I am doing. So, anyway, how was work today?"

"I should be asking you that about school," he answered. "You seem like you have something bothering you. Is that why you were looking for Mom at the store? Did you want to talk to her?"

Continued on the next page ➔

Continued from the previous page

Jessica wanted to say yes, because that would make it easier to just talk about her test score. She didn't want to have to hide anything from her father. She just knew it would take her a long time to explain it. Then, it would take that much longer to go through it all again with her mother. Jessica stared out the window. Maybe she was just thinking up excuses for not telling her dad because she knew she should. She looked at him and started to open her mouth to tell him.

Why do you think Jessica feels nervous? What can you infer about her situation?

Suddenly, a car swerved in front of them. Her dad slammed on the brakes and honked his horn. "Watch it, buddy!" he yelled at the careless driver. "You have to be so careful these days. That guy almost swerved right into us! I wonder what he was doing in that car that was more important than watching the road!"

Jessica looked down at her backpack. Maybe now was not the best time to tell her dad. Maybe she should wait at least until they got out of the car.

As they pulled into the parking lot of the grocery store, her dad took the closest spot he could find and stopped the car. "Now tell me what's bothering you, little buddy," said Jessica's dad, "because I know your mind won't be able to rest until you do."

Why can't Jessica tell her mother the problem?

Apply It

Read the passage. Think about how the details of the text help you to analyze the story and draw inferences. Answer the questions that follow.

adapted from

Heidi

by Johanna Spyri

"I want to see what you have inside the house," said Heidi.

"Come then!" and the grandfather rose and went before her toward the hut.

Heidi did as she was told. The old man now opened the door and Heidi stepped inside after him; she found herself in a good-size room, which covered the whole ground floor of the hut. A table and a chair were the only furniture; in one corner stood the grandfather's bed, in another was the hearth with a large kettle hanging above it; and on the further side was a large door in the wall—this was the cupboard. The grandfather opened it; inside were his clothes, some hanging up, others, a couple of shirts, and some socks and handkerchiefs, lying on a shelf; on a second shelf were some plates and cups and glasses; and on a higher one still, a round loaf, smoked meat, and cheese, for everything that Alm-Uncle needed for his food and clothing was kept in this cupboard. Heidi, as soon as it was opened, ran quickly forward and thrust in her bundle of clothes, as far back behind her grandfather's things as possible, so that they might not easily be found again. She then looked carefully round the room, and asked, "Where am I to sleep, grandfather?"

"Wherever you like," he answered.

Heidi was delighted, and began at once to examine all the nooks and corners to find out where it would be pleasantest to sleep. In the corner near her grandfather's bed she saw a short ladder against the wall; up she climbed and found herself in the hayloft. There lay a large heap of fresh sweet-smelling hay, while through a round window in the wall she could see right down the valley.

"I shall sleep up here, grandfather," she called down to him, "It's lovely, up here. Come up and see how lovely it is!"

"Oh, I know all about it," he called up in answer.

"I am getting the bed ready now," she called down again, as she went busily to and fro at her work, "but I shall want you to bring me up a sheet; you can't have a bed without a sheet, you want it to lie upon."

Continued on the next page ➔

Continued from the previous page

"All right," said the grandfather, and presently he went to the cupboard, and after rummaging about inside for a few minutes he drew out a long, coarse piece of stuff, which was all he had to do duty for a sheet. He carried it up to the loft, where he found Heidi had already made quite a nice bed. She had put an extra heap of hay at one end for a pillow, and had so arranged it that, when in bed, she would be able to see comfortably out through the round window.

Heidi had got hold of the sheet, but it was almost too heavy for her to carry; this was a good thing, however, as the close thick stuff would prevent the sharp stalks of the hay running through and pricking her. The two together now spread the sheet over the bed, and where it was too long or too broad, Heidi quickly tucked it in under the hay. It looked now as tidy and comfortable a bed as you could wish for, and Heidi stood gazing thoughtfully at her handiwork.

Answer these questions about *Heidi*. Write your answers in complete sentences.

1. What is Heidi doing during the story?

2. How can you describe the home that Heidi's grandfather lives in?

3. Why do you think Heidi is concerned about where she will sleep? Make an inference.

4. Why does Heidi's grandfather help her to make a comfortable bed? Make an inference.

5. What do you think Heidi's overall feeling is about being at her grandfather's house?

Figurative and Connotative Meanings

Learn About It

Authors can use **figurative language**, which means the words do not mean exactly what they say. Figurative language has a **connotative meaning**. This means that the words imply, or suggest, a certain meaning. Authors use figurative language and connotative meanings to get their point across in an interesting way.

Read the passage. As you read, try to identify the figurative language and decide on its connotative meaning.

In our up-to-the-minute, modern world, information zips along at a breakneck pace. If you don't stop once in a while to take it in, you could be lost in the dust of your own competitors. So, stop goofing around and get busy learning new technologies!

Figurative Language	Connotative Meaning
Up-to-the-minute	Constantly changing
Zips	Moves very quickly
Breakneck	Very fast
Take it in	Understand it
Left in the dust	Left behind
Goofing around	Being lazy

Try It

Read the passage. Underline phrases that use figurative language. Think about the connotative meaning of each phrase you find. Use the questions to help you.

Jack and the Beanstalk

Once upon a time, a boy named Jack lived in a small village with his mother. The family was short on money, so Jack's mother sent Jack to town to sell the family cow. On his way into town, Jack came across a man.

"Why would you sell that cow for a measly few cents," said the man, "when I can buy the cow from you in trade for these five magic beans?"

Jack was not sure what to do, but he did think magical beans sounded like a gripping idea for a trade. He gave the man the cow, and took the beans home to show his mother.

"You mean to tell me that you traded our family cow for these worthless beans?" She was so angry at Jack that she chucked the beans out the window and sent Jack to his room for the night. Jack felt terrible that he had made the wrong choice. As he fell asleep, Jack wondered what it would be like to really have magic beans.

When Jack awoke the next morning, he saw something out the window that shocked and amazed him. In the place where his mother had thrown the beans was now standing a tall beanstalk that stretched high into the clouds. There was only one explanation for what his bewildered eyes saw—the beans really were magical!

Happily, Jack jumped right onto the beanstalk and began climbing it. His mother called after him, telling him not to climb, but he turned a deaf ear. Instead, he climbed and climbed until he got to the top. At the top of the clouds was a mansion with a beastly giant. The giant threatened to eat Jack, as he loved to eat little boys. But Jack was too clever. He quickly took five golden coins from the giant and scrambled back down the beanstalk to return them to his mother.

What is the connotative meaning of the figurative phrase *short on money?*

What is the connotative meaning of *he turned a deaf ear?*

Continued on the next page

Continued from the previous page

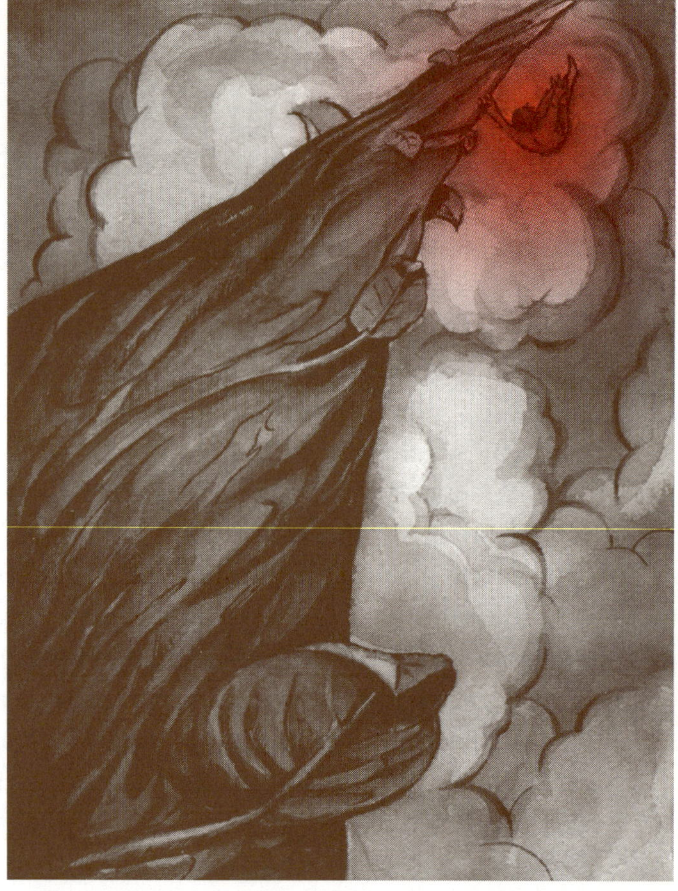

Soon, Jack decided to return to the giant's mansion again. This time, Jack spotted the giant watching a hen lay golden eggs. Jack's eyes brightened with excitement. Oh, what I could do with a hen that lays golden eggs, he thought to himself. Just then, the giant spotted Jack and again threatened to eat him. Quickly, Jack took the hen and escaped back down the beanstalk.

Jack showed the hen to his mother and they were both amazed. Jack really had traded the cow for magical beans that day when she had sent him into town. A hen that lays golden eggs could keep them rich forever! Jack and his mother spent many years selling the golden eggs from their hen. They lived like kings!

Jack decided one last time to visit the giant to see what else he might have to offer him and his family. This time, Jack took the giant's golden harp and quickly ran back down to Earth. The giant chased him down the beanstalk and almost made it out of the clouds. But, when Jack reached the bottom of the stalk, he cut it down while the giant was still on it. And that was the end of the giant.

What is the connotative meaning of the sentence "They lived like kings"?

Apply It

Read the passage. Think about how the author's use of figurative language can help you understand the connotative meaning. Answer the questions that follow.

A Dog's Tricks

The school pet show was just one week away, and Layla had not been able to make her dog do a single trick. She wondered if the dog really did know the tricks, but had secretly decided to refuse to do them. Was Rufus laughing at her behind the bushy white fur that covered his face? Every time she told him to stay, he ran. Every time she told him to sit, he chased his tail in a circle! She was ready to give him big rewards for good behavior. She planned on cheering, clapping, giving out doggie treats, and even letting him have some extra playtime each day. But she never even got the chance to hand out a single reward to him.

How could she have blown it, she wondered to herself.

"Rufus just doesn't take you seriously," claimed Layla's friend Mike. "You have to use a very firm voice with him and show him that you mean business. *You* are in charge, not him." He happily demonstrated what he meant.

"Come here, boy," he yelled in a harsh tone. Rufus just cocked his head in confusion. Mike clapped his hands like a drill sergeant. "*Come here boy*," he repeated. Rufus quickly bolted from the room.

Layla smiled. "Good job," she said. "I could really tell who was in charge that last time. I have to say, I think it was Rufus."

Mike was fuming. "You see, the next rule I was going to tell you about is that you can never give up. You have to keep working at it until you are successful." He started to run after Rufus, but Layla stopped him.

"Hold on, Mike," she said. "You know, I don't really care about winning this pet show at school next week," she admitted. "I don't want to put Rufus through all of these problems just so that I can prove to everyone that he will listen to me. He's always such a good dog and plays with me all the time. I don't care if he sits up when

Continued on the next page ➔

Continued from the previous page

I tell him to. He doesn't need to beg for a treat, either. I'm always ready to give him a treat anyway."

"Suit yourself," said Mike. "I just know that training a dog isn't as hard as some people make it seem. Dogs really like to please their masters, so they work hard at following their instructions. I trained my dog in just one weekend."

Just as they were talking, Rufus returned to the room. He could sense that they were no longer concerned with trying to make him follow orders. He lazily curled up on the couch and closed his eyes.

"It would be nice if Rufus wanted to be trained," replied Layla, "but I am not interested in making him miserable in the process. These tricks are for me, not for him. I have to think about him more and not worry about this silly pet show at school."

With that, Rufus climbed off the couch, walked up to Layla, and offered her his paw. He then sat, begged, and smiled a big, goofy Rufus smile.

Answer these questions about "A Dog's Tricks." Write your answers in complete sentences.

1. The author writes, "How could she have blown it, she wondered to herself." Which words in the sentence have a figurative meaning?

2. What is the connotative meaning of the phrase "show him that you mean business"?

3. The author writes, "Mike clapped his hands like a drill sergeant." What is the connotative meaning of the sentence?

4. In the sentence "Rufus quickly bolted from the room," which word has a figurative meaning?

5. What is the connotative meaning of the phrase "suit yourself"?

Learn About It

The **point of view** is the perspective from which a story is told. A **narrator** is someone who tells a story. The narrator can have a first-person, third-person, or a second-person point of view. A **first-person** narrator uses *I* and is usually the main character in the story. A **third-person** narrator is outside the story and uses *he* or *she*. A **second-person** narrator addresses the reader directly as *you*.

Read the passages. As you read, think about the narrators' points of view.

The crowd roared with excitement when I finished my piano solo. I was the hit of the evening, and everyone knew it. I waved at my fans and gave them a thumbs-up sign. I wanted them to know that I appreciate them, also. Anyone who comes out to see me play piano is OK in my book.

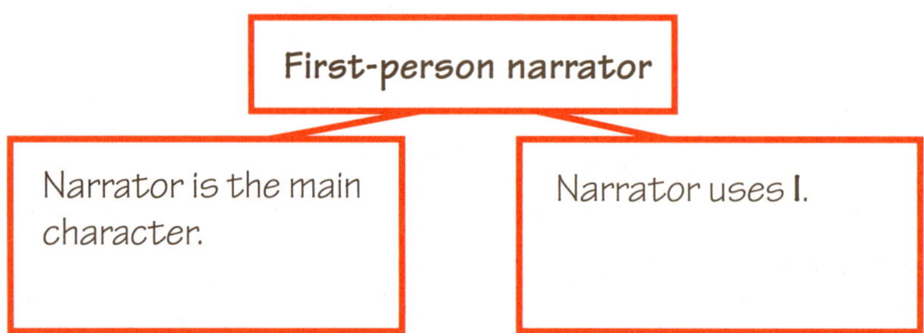

The crowd roared with excitement when Sally finished her piano solo. She was the hit of the evening, and everyone knew it. She waved at her fans and gave them a thumbs-up sign. She wanted them to know that she appreciates them, also. Anyone who comes out to see her play piano is OK in her book.

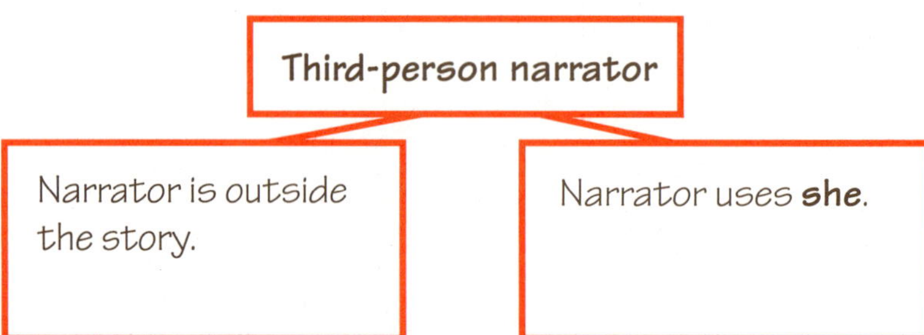

Try It

Read the passage. Underline phrases that help you determine the theme of the passage. Use the questions to help you.

adapted from

Alice in Wonderland

by Lewis Carroll

Alice was beginning to get very tired of sitting by her sister on the bank, and of having nothing to do. Once or twice she had peeped into the book her sister was reading, but it had no pictures or conversations in it. "And what is the use of a book," thought Alice, "without pictures or conversations?"

From whose point of view does the author tell the story?

So, she was considering, in her own mind, whether the pleasure of making a daisy chain would be worth the trouble of getting up and picking the daisies, when suddenly a white rabbit with pink eyes ran close by her.

There was nothing so very remarkable in that; nor did Alice think it so *very* much out of the way to hear the rabbit say to itself, "Oh dear! Oh dear! I shall be too late!" When she thought it over afterward, it occurred to her that she ought to have wondered at this, but at the time it all seemed quite natural. But, when the Rabbit actually *took a watch out of its waistcoat pocket*, and looked at it, and then hurried on, Alice started to her feet, for it flashed across her mind that she had never before seen a rabbit with either a waistcoat pocket, or a watch to take out of it, and, burning with curiosity, she ran across the field after it. She arrived just in time to see it pop down a large rabbit hole under the hedge.

In another moment, down went Alice after it, never once considering how in the world she was to get out again.

The rabbit hole went straight on like a tunnel for some way, and then dipped suddenly down, so suddenly that Alice had not a moment to think about stopping herself before she found herself falling down what seemed to be a very deep well.

Either the well was very deep, or she fell very slowly, for she had plenty of time as she went down to look about her, and to wonder what was going to happen next. First, she tried to look down and make out what she was coming to, but it was

Continued on the next page ➡

Continued from the previous page

too dark to see anything; then, she looked at the sides of the well, and noticed that they were filled with cupboards and bookshelves; here and there, she saw maps and pictures hung upon pegs. She took down a jar from one of the shelves as she passed: it was labeled "ORANGE MARMALADE," but to her great disappointment it was empty. She did not like to drop the jar, for fear of killing somebody underneath, so she managed to put it into one of the cupboards as she fell past it.

Down, down, down. Would the fall never come to an end? "I wonder how many miles I've fallen by this time?" she said aloud. "I must be getting somewhere near the center of Earth. Let me see: that would be four thousand miles down, I think—" (For, you see, Alice had learned several things of this sort in her lessons in the schoolroom, and though this was not a very good opportunity for showing off her knowledge, as there was no one to listen to her, still it was good practice to say it over.) "Yes, that's about the right distance—but then I wonder what latitude or longitude I've got to?" (Alice had not the slightest idea what *latitude* was, or *longitude* either, but she thought they were nice grand words to say.)

What is one way the author makes the character's thoughts clear to the reader?

HOTS Understand

How would the passage change if it were written with a first-person narrator?

Apply It

Read the passage. Think about the narrator's point of view. Answer the questions that follow.

My Homework

Homework has become a huge problem in my house. I am either doing homework, about to do homework, or getting in trouble for not having finished my homework. Last week, I was home sick with the flu. You would not believe how much homework I missed and had to make up after that! It's amazing that teachers can give students so much homework. I spent nearly a week making up for homework and also doing the new homework that was piling up on top of it!

My mother said that homework is an important part of learning, but I am not so sure that is true. I listen in class, and I understand what is being said. I don't think that practice upon practice is needed for me to master this stuff. I think the teacher can give us more tests to find out whether we understand what is being taught, and a lot less homework.

For example, when I learned how to do long division, I had to do about 150 practice problems over the course of the unit. Sure, they were a little hard at first and then they got easier to do, but I feel like I wasted so much of my time, I can't even tell you.

It's not that I am completely against homework. I think it can help people when they don't understand something. But we just get so much homework every night that I barely have time for anything else.

When my older sister went to this school, she used to say the same thing about homework. Now she is in high school, and she always tells me that I will be glad I got used to homework at my age. She says that there is a lot of homework in high school, and there is no way around it. She always wishes that she were back in sixth grade like me. It's funny that I think it's so terrible, and she thinks it was great. I guess people like to complain about whatever situation they are in at the time. I am no exception. It is hard to appreciate the homework you get while you are in the middle of doing it. Instead, I think most people like to complain and wish that they didn't have to do things they don't want to do.

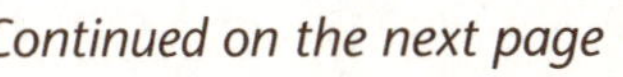

Continued on the next page

Continued from the previous page

I guess I would never understand this unless I heard my sister talk about being in the sixth grade. She had such fond memories that she made me think about my own younger years. I thought back to second grade when I barely had any homework at all. I wish I could go back to that fun time. I do remember thinking at the time that learning to read was really hard. I guess I overcame that, though, because now I am a great reader. Maybe it is the same with homework. Maybe I will just get used to it. It's funny how our opinion changes depending on what we are going through.

Answer these questions about "My Homework." Write your answers in complete sentences.

1. Who is the narrator of the story?

2. From what point of view is the story told? How do you know?

3. How does the author develop the narrator's point of view?

4. How would the point of view change if the sister were the narrator?

5. How would the passage change if it were written in second-person point of view?

Word Choice and Tone

Learn About It

Word choice can affect the meaning of a story, and it can also affect the tone. **Tone** is the quality of a passage. The tone of a passage can be *excited, silly, serious,* or *angry*. The words of the characters help set the tone. The narrator's attitude and word choices also set the tone. The tone of a passage can change. Tone depends on the actions and feelings of the characters. It also depends on the way the plot develops.

Read the passage. As you read, try to decide what the tone of the story is.

Abigail peeked eagerly out the window. The snow had already started to fall. She could barely control herself. She let out a squeal of happiness and then covered her own mouth tightly. She quietly snuck back into bed and pulled the covers up to her shoulders. Snow day, she thought to herself happily.

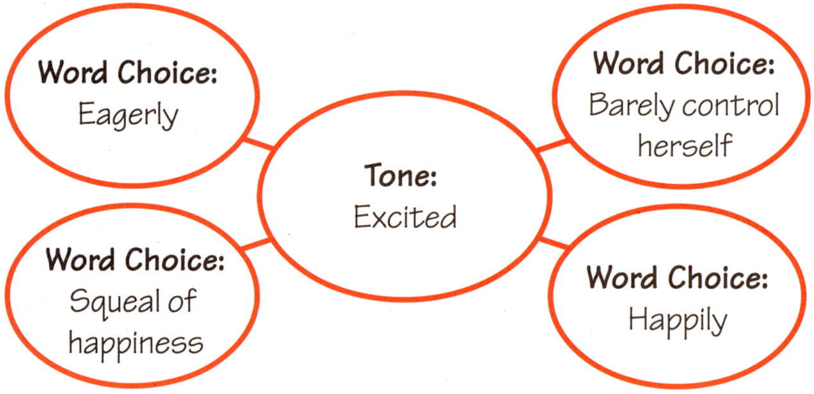

Try It

Read the passage. Underline words or phrases that help you determine the tone of the passage. Use the questions to help you.

adapted from

The Adventures of Peter Pan

by James M. Barrie

All children, except one, grow up. They soon know that they will grow up, and the way Wendy knew was this: One day, when she was two years old, she was playing in a garden, and she plucked another flower and ran with it to her mother. I suppose she must have looked rather delightful, for Mrs. Darling put her hand to her heart and cried, "Oh, why can't you remain like this forever!" This was all that passed between them on the subject, but Wendy knew that she must grow up. You always know after you are two. Two is the beginning of the end.

Wendy came first to the home of Mr. and Mrs. Darling, then John, then Michael.

How does the author set the tone of the passage?

For a week or two after Wendy came, it was doubtful whether they would be able to keep her, as she was another mouth to feed. Mr. Darling was frightfully proud of her, but he was very practical, and he sat on the edge of Mrs. Darling's bed, holding her hand and calculating expenses, while she looked at him with begging eyes. She wanted to risk it, come what might, but that was not his way; his way was with a pencil and a piece of paper, and if she confused him with suggestions he had to begin at the beginning again.

Continued on the next page ➡

Continued from the previous page

"Now, don't interrupt," he would beg of her.

"I have one pound seventeen here, and two and six at the office; I can cut off my coffee at the office, say ten shillings, making two nine and six, with your eighteen and three makes three nine seven, with five zero zero in my checkbook makes eight nine seven—who is that moving?—eight nine seven, dot and carry seven—don't speak, my own—and the pound you lent to that man who came to the door—quiet, child—dot and carry child—there, you've done it!—did I say nine nine seven? Yes, I said nine nine seven; the question is, can we try it for a year on nine nine seven?"

How does the narrator's tone compare to Mr. Darling's tone?

"Of course we can, George," she cried. But she was prejudiced in Wendy's favor, and he was really the grander character of the two.

"Remember mumps," he warned her, almost threateningly, and off he went again. "Mumps one pound, that is what I have put down, but I daresay it will be more like thirty shillings—don't speak—measles one five, German measles half a guinea, makes two fifteen six—don't waggle your finger—whooping-cough, say fifteen shillings"—and so on it went, and it added up differently each time; but at last Wendy just got through, with mumps reduced to twelve six, and the two kinds of measles treated as one.

There was the same excitement over John, and Michael had even a narrower squeak; but both were kept, and soon, you might have seen the three of them going in a row to Miss Fulsom's kindergarten school, accompanied by their nurse.

Which word choices might show you that the tone could also be comical?

Apply It

Read the passage. Think about how word choices help you decide on the tone of the passage. Answer the questions that follow.

Ready to Ride

Anita was fearful as she walked up to the roller-coaster door. "Go on," said Netavia, as she nudged her toward the seat. "Climb in. I'll be right there next to you. It's not bad at all." Anita didn't quite believe her friend that a roller coaster called "The Scream" was "not bad at all."

"I don't think so, Netavia," said Anita. "Maybe I can try again later." Anita rushed out of the line and sat down on a nearby bench. Other people in line rushed in to fill the space she left. Netavia reluctantly left the line as well, so that she could be with her friend. She sat down next to Anita.

Ever since Anita was six years old, she refused to go near the amusement park rides her friends were going on. With an amusement park so close to her house, it had become a problem over the years. Going to the Fun House Amusement Park in her town was a common activity for summer weekends, birthday parties, and play dates. But Anita wished the amusement park did not even exist. Every time she went, there was a reminder of how scared she was of most of the rides. The Scream was probably the worst one, in her mind. Its unexpected twists, hairpin turns, and sudden drops and jolts were more than she could bear. Anita had never been on the ride herself, but she had seen it in action countless times. Her friends had been begging her to go on the ride for years, but Anita had never given in to the pressure. She had walked up to the roller coaster's entry gate about fifty times. Each time she chickened out at the end and went scrambling to the very bench she was sitting on with Netavia.

Why was she the only one who was afraid of the roller coaster? Why didn't other people think about the possible dangers of being jostled around on the ride? Everyone she knew thought it was fun to go fast and be whipped around like a rag doll.

Continued on the next page ➜

Continued from the previous page

Netavia broke the silence in the air as she interrupted a jumble of Anita's thoughts. "Listen," said Netavia. "Come try it just once, and I promise I will never bother you about it again. How could I bother you again if you really tried, right?"

Anita looked up at her friend. Netavia had been so patient with her about her fears. Maybe she should just give it a try for Netavia. "You promise you'll never bother me again?" Anita said, glaring at her friend.

"Promise," Netavia assured her.

"OK, then," said Anita reluctantly. She rose from the bench and took a small step toward the back of the line. "You have been a good friend about this. You have never forced me or made fun of me. If I do it for anyone, it will definitely be for you," said Anita with a smile.

Answer these questions about "Ready to Ride." Write your answers in complete sentences.

1. What is the narrator's tone?

____

____

2. How do Anita's feelings and actions add to the tone of the passage?

____

____

3. Which words from the passage help tell you about the tone?

____

____

4. What happens in the plot that makes Anita change her actions?

____

____

5. How does the passage's tone change from the beginning to the end?

____

____

LESSON 9

Poem Structure

Learn About It

A **poem** is a kind of writing that has rhythm when read or spoken aloud. Poems are written in **lines**. A group of lines make up a **stanza**. Each stanza is a separate thought, similar to a paragraph. Some poems tell stories. The lines and stanzas contribute to the development of the **setting**, **theme**, or **plot**.

Read the stanza. As you read, try to decide how the lines fit within the stanza.

My friend came out to play today—
It's breakfast time for her—
She hunts along the woods each day,
Berries and seeds stuck in her fur.

Line of Poem	How It Fits in the Stanza
My friend came out to play today—	Introduces topic or characters
It's breakfast time for her—	Sets the tone and describes the scene
She hunts along the woods each day,	Describes the action and setting
Berries and seeds stuck in her fur.	Reveals details about the character

Try It

Read the poem. Underline lines that seem most important to the overall poem. Use the questions to help you.

adapted from

The Haunted Palace

by Edgar Allan Poe

In the greenest of our valleys
By good angels occupied,
Once a fair and stately palace—
Radiant palace—reared its head.
In the monarch Thought's dominion—
It stood there!
Never angel spread a wing
Over fabric half so fair!

Banners yellow, glorious, golden,
On its roof did float and flow,
(This—all this—was in the olden
Time long ago),
And every gentle air that lingered,
In that sweet day,
Along the ramparts white and clouded,
A winged odor went away.

Wanderers in that happy valley,
Through two shining windows, saw
Spirits moving musically,
To a lute's well-tuned law,
Bound about a throne where, sitting
(As if butterflies)
In state his glory well befitting,
The ruler of the realm was seen.

How many stanzas does this poem have?

How many lines does each stanza have?

Continued on the next page ➔

Continued from the previous page

And all with pearl and ruby glowing
Was the fair palace door,
Through which came flowing, flowing, flowing,
And sparkling evermore,
A troop of Echoes, whose sweet duty
Was but to sing,
In voices of surpassing beauty,
The wit and wisdom of their king.

But evil things, in robes of sorrow,
Attacked the monarch's high estate.
(Ah, let us mourn!—for never morrow
Shall dawn upon him desolate!)
And round about his home the glory
That blushed and bloomed,
Is but a dim-remembered story
Of the old time entombed.

And travelers, now, within that valley,
Through the red-lighted windows see
Vast forms, that move fantastically
To a discordant melody,
While, like a ghastly rapid river,
Through the pale door
A hideous throng rush out forever
And laugh—but smile no more.

HOTS Analyze

How does the speaker feel about the palace? Which lines help you support your inference?

Apply It

Read the poem. Think about how the lines and stanzas fit into the overall poem. Answer the questions that follow.

excerpted and adapted from

The Bridge

by Henry Wadsworth Longfellow

I stood on the bridge at midnight,
As the clocks were striking the hour,
And the moon rose o'er the city,
Behind the dark bell-tower.

I saw her bright reflection
In the waters under me,
Like a golden goblet falling
And sinking into the sea.

Among the long, black rafters
The wavering shadows lay,
And the current that came from the ocean
Seemed to lift and bear them away;

And like those waters rushing
Among the wooden piers,
A flood of thoughts came o'er me
That filled my eyes with tears.

How often, oh, how often,
I had wished that the ebbing tide
Would bear me away on its bosom
O'er the ocean wild and wide!

For my heart was hot and restless,
And my life was full of care,
And the burden laid upon me
Seemed greater than I could bear.

But now it has fallen from me,
It is buried in the sea;
And only the sorrow of others
Throws its shadow over me.

Continued on the next page ➡

Continued from the previous page

Yet whenever I cross the river
On its bridge with wooden piers,
Like the odor of brine from the ocean
Comes the thought of other years.

And I think how many thousands
Of care-encumbered men,
Each bearing his burden of sorrow,
Have crossed the bridge since then.

I see the long procession
Still passing to and fro,
The young heart hot and restless,
And the old subdued and slow!

And forever and forever,
As long as the river flows,
As long as the heart has passions,
As long as life has woes;

The moon and its broken reflection
And its shadows shall appear,
As the symbol of love in dreamland,
And its wavering image here.

Answer these questions about "The Bridge." Write your answers in complete sentences.

1. How many stanzas are in this poem?

2. How many lines does each stanza have?

3. What is the purpose of the first stanza?

4. What does the poem describe?

LESSON 10

Drama Structure

Learn About It

A **drama** is a kind of writing that is meant to be performed as a play. A drama has characters, a plot, and a setting. The plot moves along through the use of **dialogue**, the words the characters say to each other. **Stage directions** tell the actor how to act or move. A drama is divided into **scenes**, which show a change of location or time. An **act** is a group of related scenes.

Read the list of scenes and acts for a drama below. As you read, think about how the drama will likely develop.

The Cat and the Mouse

Act I	**Friends Meet**
Scene 1	The Cat Gets Friendly
Scene 2	In the Kitchen
Scene 3	The Cupboard is Bare
Act II	**The Battle Begins**
Scene 1	The Chase
Scene 2	Into the Backyard
Scene 3	Making Up Is Hard To Do

Beginning	→	Middle	→	End
Cat and Mouse begin as friends in Act I, Scene 1.	→	They begin to fight around Act II, Scene 1.	→	Cat and Mouse make up at the end, Act II, Scene 3.

Try It

Read the drama. Underline dialogue or other words that help you follow the story and plot. Use the questions to help you.

Smell the Roses

Act I Scene 1

Setting: Curtain rises, showing a boy and his mother in a car on their way to school.

MOM: (*in a hurry*) We're late again, Raj. I think we'd better get you to bed earlier at night to make sure you get up in enough time to get to school on time. I don't want you missing any tests first thing in the morning.

RAJ: (*exhausted*) I can't believe how early we get up already, and it's not enough. I can't believe that we have to get up even earlier now. I'm exhausted every morning.

MOM: Sorry, honey. It's just a matter of getting onto a good schedule and sticking to it. When you stay up late some nights and move your schedule around, your body ends up paying for it. We can work this out, though. Don't worry. I know you will be fine once you get into a groove. Here we are. (*pulling up to school*) Have a great day, and I'll see you this afternoon.

RAJ: Thanks, Mom. I'll see you later.

Act I Scene 2

Setting: Raj alone in his bedroom doing his homework at his desk.

RAJ: (*relaxed*) This is not going to be as bad as I thought. I'm already done with most of my math, and I only have some science homework left for the night. I guess I can go to bed early tonight, after all.

What is the main problem in the drama?

(*Mom enters the room.*)

MOM: Hi, Raj. How did it go today at school? Did you get a lot of homework? Did you miss anything by being late today?

RAJ: I have the regular amount of homework tonight, but I'm almost finished already. I got an earlier start on it than usual. And no, I didn't miss anything by being late. But if I had shown up about a minute later, my social studies test would have started without me!

MOM: (*relieved*) Wow! I guess we know what we have to do tomorrow morning. We'll get out of here about ten minutes earlier, and you should be fine.

RAJ: Sounds good. I'll talk to you in the morning. Good night.

MOM: Good night.

Continued on the next page ➔

Continued from the previous page

Act I Scene 3

Setting: Raj and his mother are driving in the car on the way to school again. Same set as Scene 1.

MOM: Here we are, Raj. We're at school earlier than ever.

RAJ: (*confused*) Well, I wonder what I should do! I've never been here this early.

MOM: (*laughing*) This is the perfect opportunity to do what people all over this busy world wish every day that they can do. You actually have time to stop and smell the roses! Enjoy yourself. It's a beautiful day. Take in the morning sunshine and gather your thoughts before school.

RAJ: (*relieved*) That's actually not a bad idea, Mom. Not a bad idea at all. (*gets out of the car*) You have a good day, too, and maybe you can get some time to smell the roses also!

At what point in the drama does Raj begin to feel in control of his situation at school?

HOTS Apply

If you inserted a new scene into the play, what would it be and how would it support the main idea of the play?

Apply It

Read the drama. Think about how the scenes help you understand the drama as a whole. Answer the questions that follow.

Babysitting Problems

Act I Scene 1

Setting: Curtain rises, showing a teen girl babysitting a two-year-old and an eight-year-old boy.

BECCA: Do you boys want to play a game? We can play hide and seek if you'd like.

PEDRO: No.

JUAN: He doesn't like to play anything. He's only two. He thinks everybody should just wait on him hand and foot.

BECCA: That's OK. You don't have to play a game. We can do what you guys want. What would you like to do?

PEDRO: Paint!

JUAN: You'd better look out when he wants to paint. He's really messy. Once he poured a whole jar of paint all over the living room rug. It was so funny. I laughed like crazy.

PEDRO: Paint! Now!

BECCA: (*concerned*) OK, Pedro. If you want to paint, then we can. But your brother says that you can be a little messy sometimes. How about if we just do a little watercolor and try to be as neat as we can?

PEDRO: Paint!

JUAN: I'll go get the paints.

BECCA: Thanks. I think.

Act I Scene 2

Setting: A kitchen, with large watercolor paintings strewn around.

BECCA: (*relieved*) Oh, Pedro, you're a great artist. I am so proud of your work, and especially with how neat you were while you were painting. We can put all of these paintings up to dry and put the paints away before your parents get home.

(*Pedro stands up on kitchen chair.*)

PEDRO: No, stop! More, more!!

Continued on the next page ➡

Continued from the previous page

(*Juan rolls his eyes.*)

BECCA: I'm sorry, Pedro. It's time to start cleaning up. We have to start getting you ready for bed. Would you like to hear a bedtime story?

PEDRO: (*defiant*) No! Still paint! Still paint!

JUAN: Pedro, you're going to get in trouble if you don't listen to Becca. And I'm definitely going to tell Mom and Dad on you.

PEDRO: No bed! Paint! Paint! Paint! (*begins to run around room with paintbrushes in his hands, flicking paint all around him*)

BECCA: No, Pedro! Come back! I can let you paint one more painting if you stop running around with those brushes!

PEDRO: (*stops in his tracks*) Paint one more?

BECCA: (*desperate*) Yes, come sit here, and I'll help you do one more. Juan, help me get these papers, paints, and brushes picked up. Your parents will be here any minute.

JUAN: OK. (*quickly collects painting materials*) But there's paint everywhere!

BECCA: I know. We'll work fast. (*perks up to hear key jiggling in the front door*)

PARENTS: (*calling from off stage*) Hello, kids! We're home!

(Becca looks at audience with comic despair.)

Curtain falls.

Answer these questions about "Babysitting Problems." Write your answers in complete sentences.

1. Who are the main characters in the drama?

____

____

2. What is the main problem in the drama?

____

____

3. Why was it important to have a scene change in the drama?

____

____

4. What happens when Pedro runs around the room with the paintbrushes?

____

____

5. How do the stage directions help the author to tell the story?

____

____

LESSON 11

Compare and Contrast Stories and Poems

Learn About It

When you **compare and contrast** stories and poems, you tell how they are *alike* and *different*. For example, a poem and a story can have a similar **theme** or **topic**. However, they may be written in very different ways. A story will have a plot and characters. A poem may focus on feelings or sensory details.

Read the story and the poem. As you read, try to decide how the poem and story are alike and different.

Story

Martin burst open the doors to the school and ran out into the warm sunshine with the other children. Summer vacation had begun!

Poem

The green garden is buzzing and strong.
Flowers will grow there all summer long!

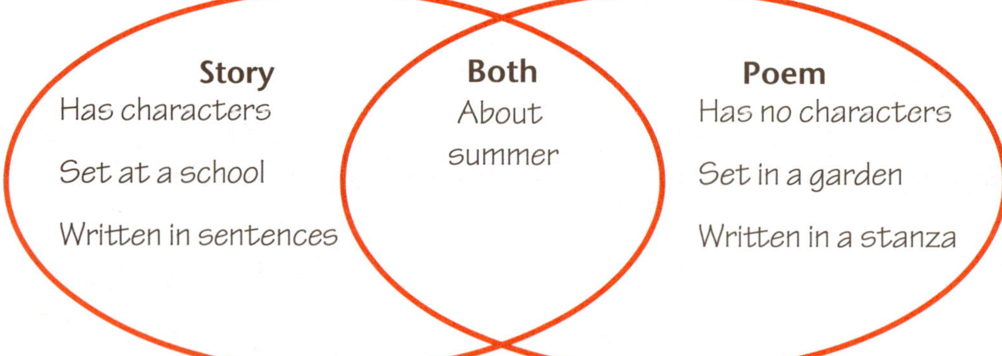

Try It

Read the story and the poem. Underline text that helps you compare and contrast the texts. Use the questions to help you.

Saturday Mornings

Every Saturday, my best friend, Jenny, always asks me to go play soccer with her early in the morning. And just about every Saturday morning, I tell Jenny that I would rather snuggle warm in my bed and relax.

I know that my puppy, Truffles, feels the same way about Saturday mornings. She is always up at the crack of dawn, but then she soon snuggles up to me under the covers and falls back to sleep. She must know it's Saturday morning and time for the house to relax. It's one of the only days I don't have to get up and hurry to school.

What is the story about?

Sometimes I think Truffles understands me more than anyone on Earth. I certainly understand her more than anyone else. Sometimes I think I should have been born as a dog instead of a human. I understand the lifestyle of a dog more than the lifestyle of a human. If I could be a dog, I would know just what to do every day and every night. I would play, sleep, play, and then sleep. And that would bring me into the next day when I would do it all over again. I don't think there is anything more important in the world than play and sleep. A dog knows that. Why can't people learn that, too?

Maybe Truffles is my best friend in the world. People call dogs *man's best friend.* I don't think anyone has ever had a friend as good as Truffles, human or not.

excerpted from

Puppy and I

by A.A. Milne

I met a horse as I went walking;
We got talking,
Horse and I.
"Where are you going to, Horse, today?"
(I said to the Horse as he went by.)
"Down to the village to get some hay.
Will you come with me?"
"No, not I."

I met some Rabbits as I went walking;
We got talking,
Rabbits and I.
"Where are you going in your brown fur coats?"
(I said to the Rabbits as they went by.)
"Down to the village to get some oats.
Will you come with us?"
"No, not I."

I met a Puppy as I went walking;
We got talking,
Puppy and I.
"Where are you going this nice fine day?"
(I said to the Puppy as he went by.)
"Up to the hills to roll and play."
"I'll come with you, Puppy," said I.

What do the story and poem have in common?

How are the story and poem different from each other?

Which part of the story would you change to make it even more similar to the poem?

Apply It

Read the story and the poem. Compare and contrast the theme and topic of the texts. Answer the questions that follow.

The Willow Wife

In a small Japanese village grew a large willow tree that had provided peaceful shade to villagers for years and years. Very near the willow lived a young farmer named Heitaro. He often sat in the shade of the tree, and he felt that he knew the calm spirit of the great tree better than any other villager.

A few villagers came to Heitaro's house one evening. They told him of their need for a bridge over the river. They wanted to use the willow wood because it was strong and hard. He offered to give three of his own trees so that the willow could be spared. The group quickly agreed.

One evening soon after, Heitaro saw a young woman under the willow. For many nights, Heitaro and the woman met under the tree and talked. One evening, he asked, "Dear lady, will you be my wife?" She sighed like the leaves of the willow in a gentle breeze. "Yes."

In time, they had a child, and the family was happy. But then the emperor decided to build a temple in Kyoto, and he needed wood. The villagers felt they should present him with their great willow. Heitaro argued. This time the people could not be swayed. It was the willow they must offer the emperor. Heitaro turned toward home, full of sorrow.

As he reached the door of his home, a piercing scream rang out. Heitaro saw his wife in agony. "Heitaro, I am the soul of the willow! The villagers are cutting and tearing me to pieces!"

In panic, Heitaro turned back toward the tree. In that instant, it fell. In despair, he turned back to his willow wife. At that moment, she disappeared.

excerpted from

The Willow-Tree

by William Makepeace Thackeray

Know you the willow-tree
Whose gray leaves quiver,
Whispering gloomily
To yon pale river;
Lady, at even-tide
Wander not near it,
They say its branches hide
A sad, lost spirit?

Once to the willow-tree
A maid came fearful,
Pale seemed her cheek to be,
Her blue eye tearful;
Soon as she saw the tree,
Her step moved fleeter,
No one was there—ah me!
No one to meet her!

Presently came the night,
Sadly to greet her,
Moon in her silver light,
Stars in their glitter;
Then sank the moon away
Under the billow,
Still wept the maid alone—
There by the willow!

Shrill blew the morning breeze,
Biting and cold,
Bleak peers the gray dawn
Over the wold.
Bleak over moor and stream
Looks the grey dawn,
Gray, with disheveled hair,
Still stands the willow there—
The maid is gone!

Answer these questions about "The Willow Wife" and "The Willow-Tree." Write your answers in complete sentences.

1. What is the theme of both the story and the poem?

___

___

2. How are topics of the story and the poem different?

___

___

3. How does the story express its theme to the reader?

___

___

___

___

4. How does the poem express its theme to the reader?

___

___

___

___

LESSON

12

Compare and Contrast Historical Fiction and Fantasy

Learn About It

Historical fiction is a story that is set in the past that uses real people, places, or events from history. A **fantasy** is a story that is not set in reality that often has characters or places with magical powers. Although historical fiction and fantasy are different types of stories, they can have similar topics and **themes**.

Read the fantasy and historical fiction passages below. As you read, try to decide how the stories are alike and different.

Fantasy

When the gnome came to life, it ran through the forest, granting everyone a wish. This is how Queen Julia got her powers to control the weather.

Historical Fiction

It hadn't rained for a while in much of the Midwest. We've had it pretty hard here in Oklahoma. Pa noticed some dark clouds in the sky a few moments ago. I thought they were rain clouds, but they were too black. Next we knew, there was dust all around.

Fantasy	Both	Historical Fiction
Not set in reality Gnome grants wishes Queen controls the weather	Deal with weather	Real events Dust Bowl Characters in danger

Try It

Read the passages. Underline phrases that help you to compare and contrast the passages. Use the questions to help you.

The Family Store

William loved working for his father's business. About three years ago, William's family opened a General Store in the sleepy town of Willow Hollow. About thirty-five people lived in this town on the Iowa plains. Hundreds more corn farmers came to town from miles away to buy their goods and make the long trek home again.

How do you know this passage is historical fiction?

William's family had to make sure the store was packed with the goods that these people would need after making their long journey. The farmers and their families relied on the general store for the things they needed. William and his father would journey long distances to get the fabrics, grains, and candies that families expected when they visited the store.

"You are a good worker, William," said his father one day while they were sitting in their covered wagon, waiting for a shipment of fabric to be loaded. They gathered some food for their horses and fed them while they waited.

"I like working at the family store," William told his father. "I want to keep working there when I grow up."

What details help you know the setting of the story?

"That's fine," answered his father. "Just don't forget to finish your studies, first. I never got to finish school. I always thought that if I had more schooling I would be able to run the store even better."

"OK, Dad," William promised. "If we work hard together, we can make our business grow. I would like to help to make that happen," he said.

"Nothing would make me happier," said his dad. William loved to make his dad proud.

The Bot Center

Marco and Sophie walked into Bot Center and were nearly struck down by flying robots zooming over their heads.

"Whoa," said Marco as he ducked out of the way. "The store is busy today."

"It sure is," replied Sophie. "I think they just opened a few minutes ago, too. I wonder if there is a big sale today."

They suddenly heard a loud robot voice over the loudspeaker. "Big sale today," said the voice. "Get your robot goods at half off. Batteries, robot oil, cleaning and cooking programs, and whatever you need to make your robot work better for you."

"Oh, maybe I can buy that cooking program for my bot," said Marco. "He is such a terrible cook."

"Yes," said Sophie. "I have been looking for a program that can help my bot do laundry better. Mine has been mixing colored and white clothes, and everything that comes out is pink!"

"Well, today is the day to do it," said Marco. "I love my robot, but sometimes he does things the wrong way."

"I know," said Sophie. "Mine, too. I hope the bots that work here know what they are doing."

Then, the lights in the store suddenly went off, music stopped, and all bots fell to the floor. Some bots flying overhead had parachutes that were suddenly activated to help them cushion their fall. The store was quiet and still.

"That is so frustrating," said Marco. "If you want to do something right, I guess you have to just do it yourself. Let's go home and do our own cooking and laundry."

"I guess you're right," said Sophie, disappointed.

HOTS Understand

How do the themes of the two stories compare?

Apply It

Read the passages. Compare and contrast the passages by their topic and theme. Answer the questions that follow.

A Winter at Valley Forge

Well, here we are in a place called Valley Forge. General Washington tells us this is a great location for many reasons. The first is that we're just twenty-five miles away from Philadelphia. We can keep the British at bay and prevent them from launching any sneak attacks on that city. Second, we're also able to keep the British from getting deeper into Pennsylvania.

We marched in—if I may say *marched.* After all, most of the men were starving or sick and could hardly walk. In any event, we arrived at camp in the middle of December. We made a proper hut for the general, but the other huts were made hastily. The huts keep out most of the cold, but the wetness lingers. The snow melts and turns to water. Then the temperature plummets and turns that water into ice. Then it snows again and melts all over again.

Many of the men remain ill, and more and more become ill with each passing day. If it were not for the talents of Baker General Christopher Ludwig, we'd all be eating nothing but fire cakes. These are nothing but tasteless mixtures of flour and water. Our starvation seems solvable, but I fear we can do nothing about all the disease around us.

I am finding it hard not to despair. After all, I even overheard General Washington saying that this army must "starve, dissolve, or disperse."

The Knights' Quest

The knights huddled around the campfire. The king had sent them on a quest to recover his crown from a giant eagle that had swooped down and stolen it while the king played croquet. The king saw the eagle fly north, but he knew not where exactly it landed. The king chose his three bravest knights to search the kingdom for the crown.

The knights searched for weeks. They did not think it would take so long to track down a giant eagle. The knights soon started to run low of food and water.

"How much food have we left?" asked Sir David.

"I have one slice of bread," answered Sir Gerald.

"Then that's all we have," said Sir Michael. "I have nothing left."

"I wish there were a farm nearby," said Sir David, as he rubbed his hands over the fire.

The other two knights made the same wish as they rubbed their hands over the fire as well.

Just then they heard a cow low in the distance. Sir David stood up and looked north. He saw a light. It seemed their wish had come true. The men packed up their stuff and went toward the light.

The knights walked for about an hour when they came to a farm. The farmer offered them hot soup and a place to sleep for the night. The men were grateful. When they woke in the morning, there was no sign of the farmer, the cow, or even the farm. But lying at their feet was the king's crown.

Answer these questions about "A Winter at Valley Forge" and "The Knights' Quest." Write your answers in complete sentences.

1. What kind of passage is "A Winter at Valley Forge"? How do you know?

____

____

2. What kind of passage is "The Knights' Quest"? How do you know?

____

____

3. How do the men in both stories get the food they need?

____

____

4. How are the stories alike?

____

____

____

____

5. How are the stories different?

____

____

____

____

Graphic Organizers

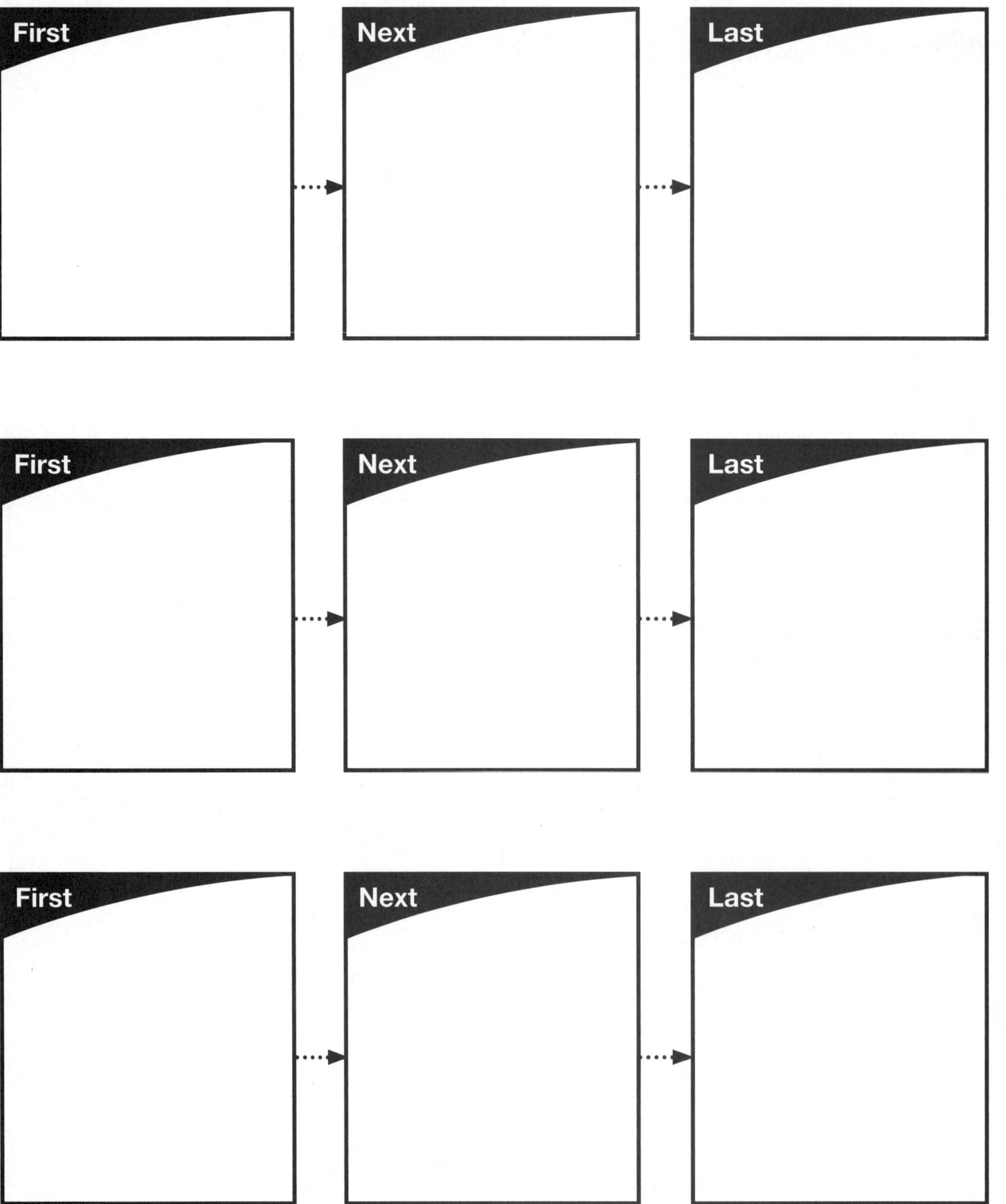

Detail
Detail
Detail
Main Idea

Main Idea
Detail
Detail

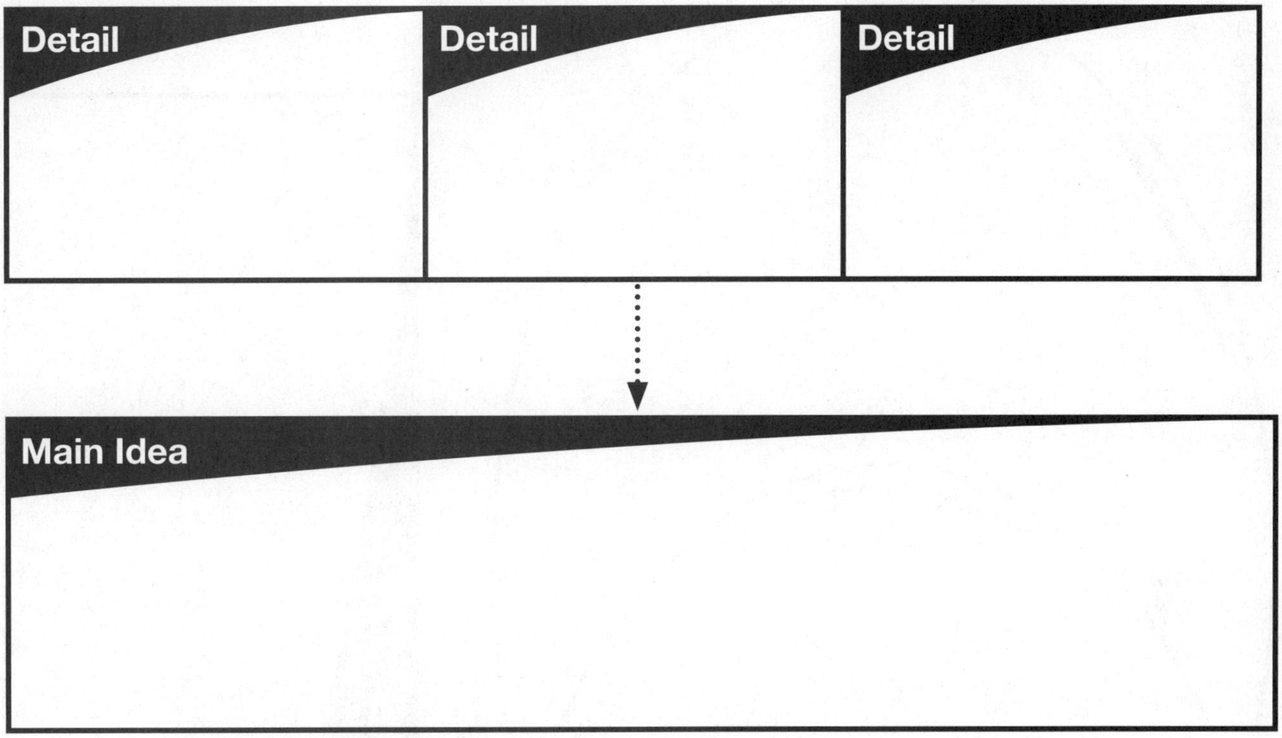

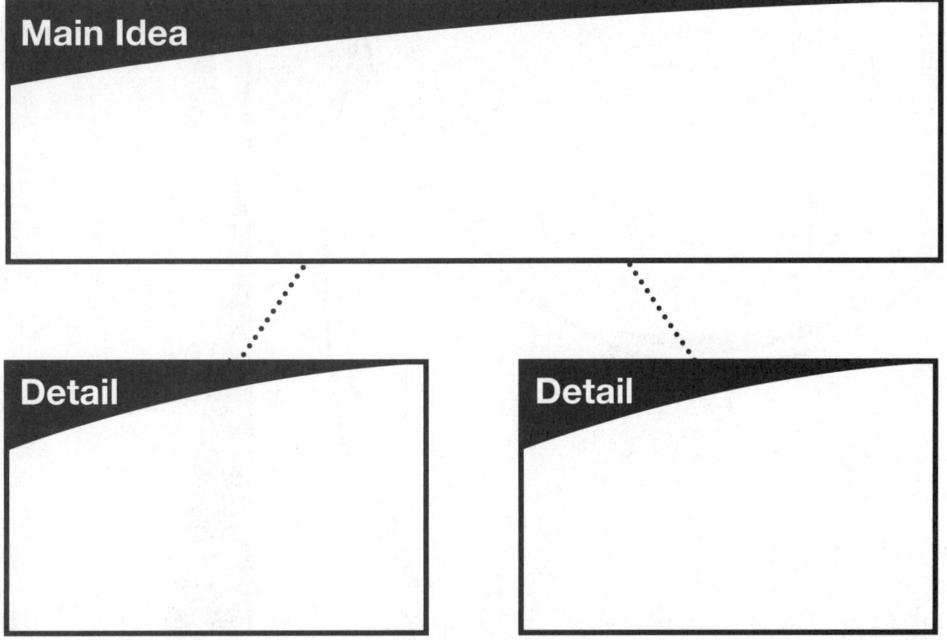

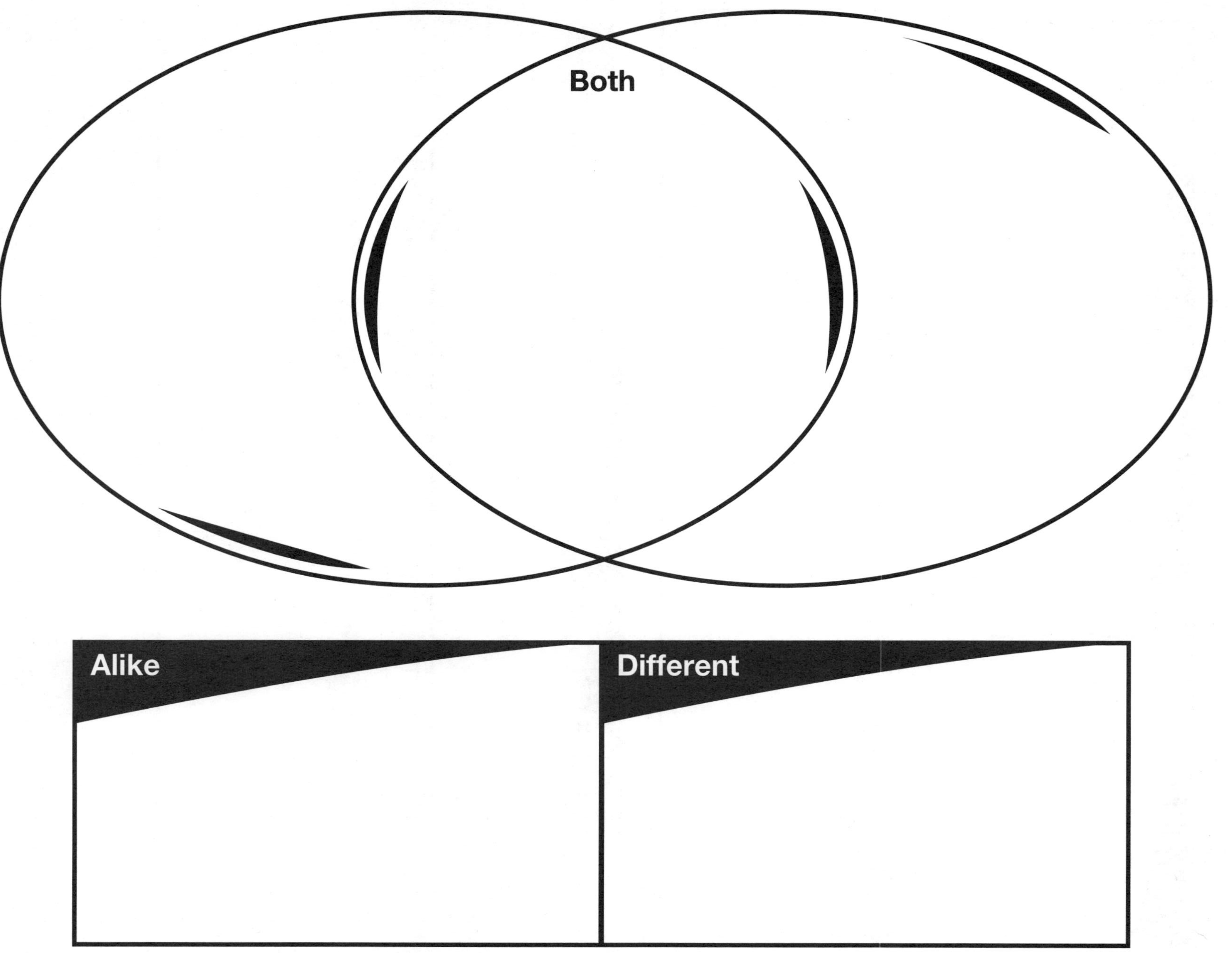
Both
Alike
Different

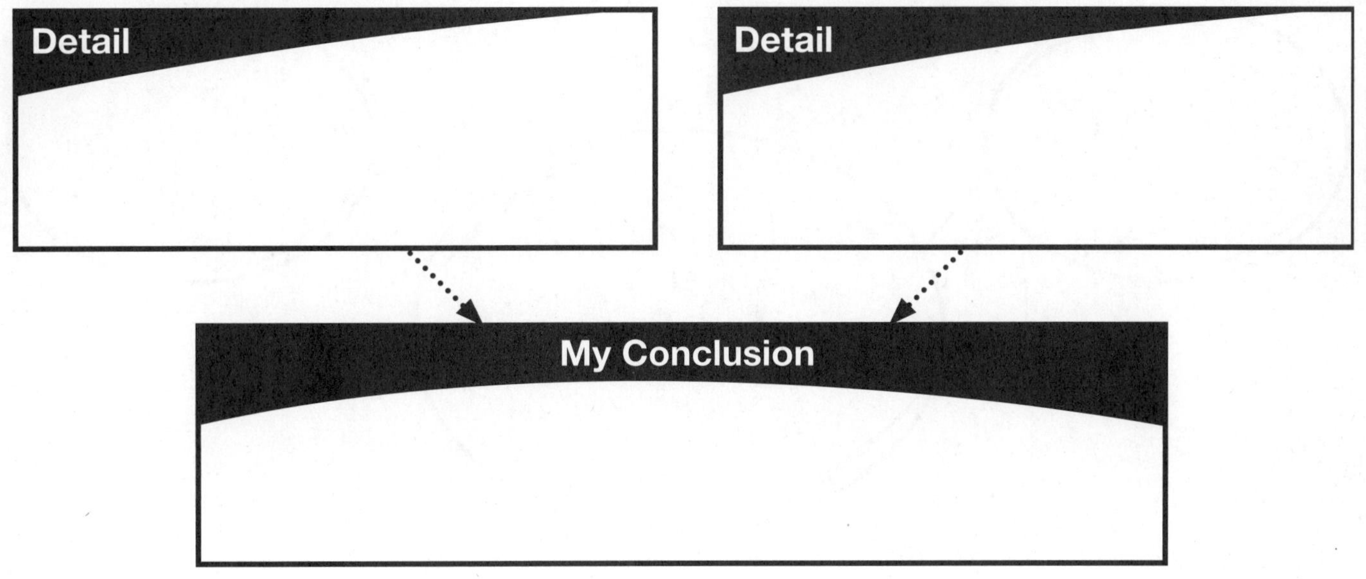
Detail
Detail
My Conclusion

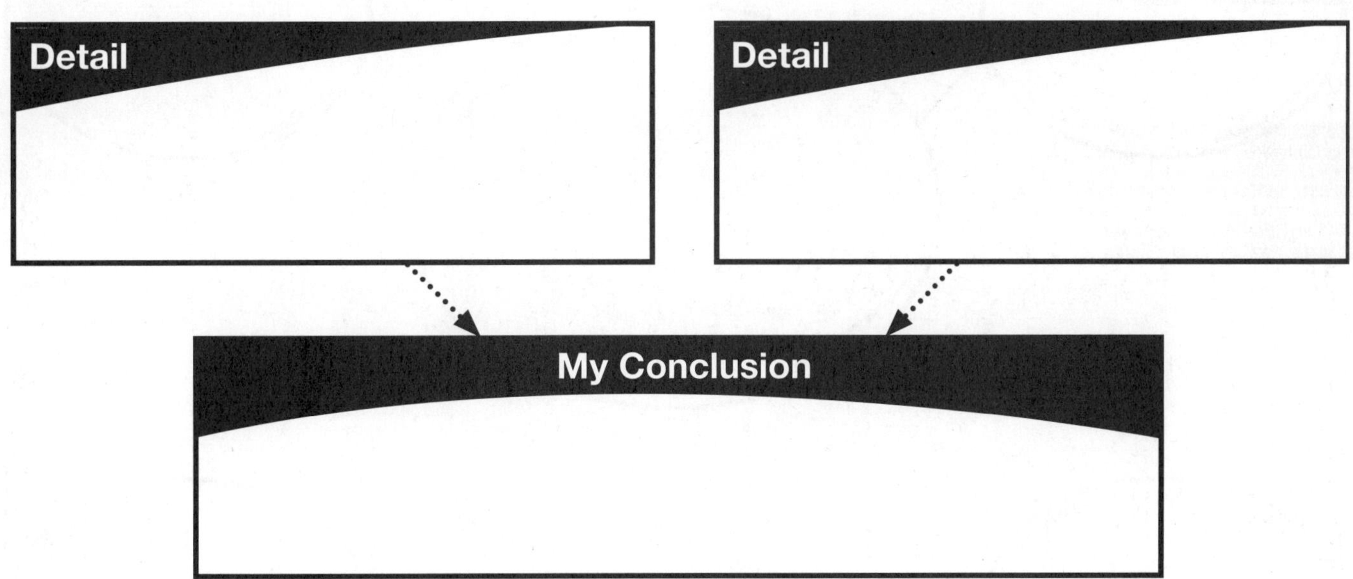
Detail
Detail
My Conclusion

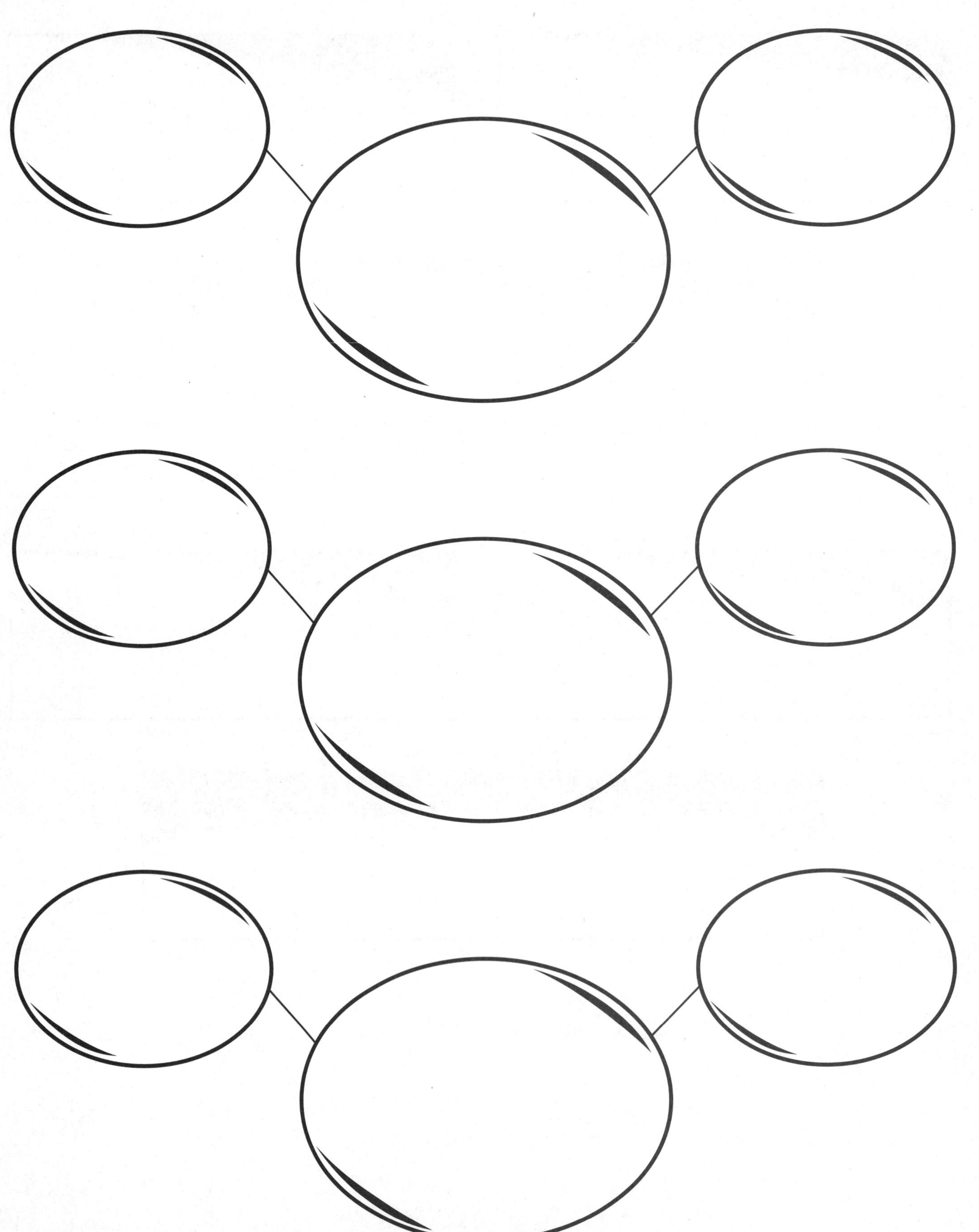